We Think We

Own It!

A Journey Towards Sustainability

Tommy Treacy

To John Meagher

ACKNOWLEDGEMENTS

The idea for this book first began to crystallise in my mind and heart when John Meagher made that comment about Eden back in 2016, as I drove through the meandering Tipperary/Waterford country roads... thanks for your inspiring intellect John, and may you rest in peace.

Writing this book has been a challenge and a joy, and I am extremely grateful to the many people who have given me so much support and encouragement.

I would like to thank Anna Jaszel, Des Marnane, Denis Coffey, Donie Hickey, Pat Carrig and Fr Jim Doyle for proof reading and suggesting changes to the many drafts I produced.

I would like to thank Michael Ryan, my former English teacher in the Abbey C.B.S. Tipperary Town, who advised me on grammatical issues from time to time.

Paddy Quinlan, Martin Breen Court, Tipperary Town, was a great man to bounce ideas off throughout the journey of this book. I thank Paddy for his wisdom and guidance, as we drank the odd drop of whiskey, while social distancing.

I fondly recall the insight into the character of Judas I received from my late uncle Connie Ryan, a Pallottine Priest. With warmth in my heart, I recall the good days and the great conversations... may you rest in peace Connie.

I would like to thank my brother Connie who assisted me when taking the photo in Miley's meadow Foildearg, during the Summer of 2021.

Thank you to my editor Aya Shappel and publisher Orla Kelly for their patience, help, direction and advice, in helping me bring this book's journey to it's destination.

Finally, I would like to thank my family, who have always lovingly supported and encouraged me in all I have done.

CONTENTS

ABSTRACT

You are about to embark on a journey... a journey that will have its trials, intrigue, mystery, insight and discovery... a journey that can ultimately take you towards a sustainable planet. The journey begins in the mythological/theological Garden of Eden and finishes deep within the human heart, similar to the journey Judas took (in spite of his many glaring faults and failings).

It is my belief, that this pathway or *road less travelled*[1], will only prove fruitful, if you experience a change of heart (metanoia), a change in behaviour and lifestyle (where you consume less energy), along with the elimination of any delusional thoughts that you might have had of ever owning the planet.

This book engages with many disciplines and areas of thought, education and art, ranging from mythology to the fundamentals of hard science, as I suggest reasons, using hypothetical thought and theoretical fact, as to why the earth is heating up, while proposing possible solutions to the crisis.

The seeds of the dark human traits of misleading others, in the quest and desire for wealth and property, shall be investigated using the mythological/theological story of Eden... traits that makes us think that we own the planet. In my opinion, this delusionary thought is one of the issues that fans global warming.

---

[1] Peck, M., S.

We Think We Own It!

I shall ponder the mystery of God and whether belief in God and prayer might help to overcome global warming, with an emphasis on devotion to Our Lady of Holy Hope.

Inspired by Bruce Springsteen, Andrea Corr, Roy Keane, David Bowie (RIP) and his wife Iman, the crew of Apollo 8 and Yuri Gagarin, I realise that some of humanity can play a crucial part in overcoming global warming, through Christian prayer and faith in God.

Inspired by the words and thoughts of Jim Stynes (RIP), I expand my thoughts to include others... even if their belief system is non-Christian.

I shall turn to philosophy as a possible solution... and Jean-Jacques Rousseau's thoughts on innate human goodness (something we are all born with), while the challenge is to remain good despite life's influences and experiences.

In conclusion, I shall refer to what I believe to be the crux of the problem that fans global warming, a crux we could say is written in the stars and can be overcome by prayer or philosophy, or both.

This journey draws to its destination with a clear strategy... however; it is a strategy under a cloud... a cloud that acknowledges the major journey the Superpowers (USA, Russia, China and others) of this planet still have to take, in order to allow truth to flow freely through their human hearts.

Greta Thunberg has already taken this journey, as she passionately speaks with truth freely flowing through her heart, and shows emotional connectedness, in how she is prepared to speak out with total honesty and openness, regarding the global warming crisis.

My concluding chapter was written the day after President Joe Biden's Inauguration ceremony. Soren Kierkegaard's statement regarding living life in a forward direction, while understanding it afterwards, resonated well with how the structure and thought process of this book, foretold President Biden's slant on what becoming President of the United States meant to him.

I now invite you to come on board and journey with me towards a hope filled future, full of grace, light, fresh air and seasonally normal mean temperatures. A future where we will all look out for and warmly salute each other with open truthful hearts, as truthful and honest as the heart of the remorseful Judas, which will reflect the spirit of the greenery of Eden.

INTRODUCTION

As I began writing this book, I did so as the typical scientist... typical teacher. I thought I had a clear plan, I thought I knew the steps I was about to take, and I thought I had a clear idea where my journey would end.

Indeed, my main aim was to write a small book, with no more than 10,000 words.

Now that I have finished, I must humbly confess that the conclusion I arrived at was not planned. It slowly surfaced and as it did, I became pleasantly surprised as to the shape it took, especially when I ended up pondering the inner heart of Judas, as he stepped away from the mob approximately 2,000 years ago... and of course I wrote in excess of 10,000 words!

On starting chapter 13, I thought I was beginning the final chapter. However, by the time I had the book finished, I had added another four chapters.

As I finished chapter 13, a new pathway opened up, as I went deeper into the subject.

As I continued writing, I began to broaden my outlook, by including the proportion of humanity that does not believe in God.

Then, I pondered innate human goodness, something I believe we are all born with... as I included the philosophical writings of Rousseau.

Inspired by Gavin James, I wrote about the importance of meaning and truth.

As this new pathway widened, I investigated truth more deeply, with a special focus on the trial of the historical Jesus. In my imagination, I stepped back in time and stood in the silence that descended on the crowd who witnessed this trial as I attempted to make sense of it all.

This trial of a totally honest and truthful man who did no wrong in his life, was unfortunately one of the many unjust moments in the history of humanity... moments that continue in today's world of the 21st century.

I pondered Jesus' reaction to this gross injustice, as He decided not to waste His precious breath attempting to defend the false accusations made against Him.

As I continued... the journey I set out on towards sustainability, became a journey deep into the mysterious human heart.

As I descended deeper, I began to realise that the crowd who witnessed Jesus being condemned to death had experienced a type of paralysis... a paralysis of their hearts... a paralysis that resulted in a blockage of truth, a paralysis that caused them to act as an inhumane mob, devoid of feelings and empathy.

In this state of paralysis they went silent, as they became emotionally disconnected from the events unfolding before their eyes, events fuelled by the mob they had become part of.

A Journey Towards Sustainability

This silence I speak of is unfortunately admired by many influential powerful people in this world today, people in managerial positions in Church and State. Indeed, it is sometimes observed as a type of wisdom... a shrewd, emotionally frozen wisdom... a wisdom where people suffer neglect and hurt... a "wisdom" where the planet earth suffers greatly.

I believe that this silence is dark... as dark as the serpent of Eden...

It is a silence where truth and honesty are absent and a hardness of heart is present, a silence where apologies are non-existent. However, this same silence was crushed by the far from perfect, yet remorseful Judas, (Jesus' betrayer), moments before be breathed his last breath, because of the truth and honesty he stood for.

As I continued my journey into the human heart, I began to realise that the crux of the problem fanning global warming was found there.

So, let us begin our journey, by taking a road less travelled... and by doing so, we can begin to heal this crux. We can do this by making changes to the way we live our lives (even if this possibly involves a reduction in our own personal standard of living), while the strength and inspiration to do so may be received perhaps through Christian prayer, other world religions/beliefs or philosophy... making this planet sustainable once again... where the breath of Jesus floats gently on the breeze, the breeze of a planet that isn't owned by anyone... a planet that just simply lives.

CHAPTER 1

THE BEGINNING

One can fix anything,
if one knows where to start

Before I begin, I would like to clearly state that a little carbon dioxide is a good thing and a little greenhouse gas is essential for the life of the planet. Two of the essential greenhouse gases present in the atmosphere are water vapour (H_2O) and carbon dioxide (CO_2). If these greenhouse gases were not present in the atmosphere, the planet would be largely frozen (with temperatures plunging to about -18 °C) and it would not sustain life, as the atmosphere would not retain any heat from the sun.

Correlation between rising CO_2 levels in the atmosphere and rising average surface temperatures, was first mentioned in scientific publications by Svante Arrhenius (who was also involved in acid/base research in chemistry) back in 1896.

So, greenhouse gas concentrations and atmospheric temperature rise have been on the radar of scientists for quite some time.

We Think We Own It!

Where do the harmful gases that cause global warming come from…?

These gases… CO_2 (carbon dioxide), CH_4 (methane), N_2O (nitrous oxide), SO_x (Sulphur Oxides) and H_2O (water vapour)… have all been created as a result of human (anthropogenic) influences.

When fossil fuels are burned, CO_2 is released. Coal, turf, oil, petrol, diesel and natural gas are examples of fossil fuels.

These fuels were produced as a result of tiny sea creatures and vegetation dying, decaying and lying buried under pressure in the mud and silt of the planet for millions of years. The actions of bacteria eventually turned this material into crude oil and natural gas etc... today's fossil fuels.

Methane and carbon dioxide are produced by various industries, while cattle also produce these gases as they digest grass.

Nitrous oxide is produced by microbes in soil, as a result of the use of artificial fertilisers that contain nitrogen.

Oxides of sulphur are produced by burning fossil fuels and from the smelting of metal and other "heavy" industries.

Another term that can be used for fossil fuel is hydrocarbon. When hydrocarbons are burned in excess oxygen, the products are carbon dioxide, heat energy and water vapour.

$$C_2H_6 \ + \ O_2 \text{(excess)} \rightarrow \ 2CO_2 \ + \ 3H_2O \ + \ \text{Heat energy}$$

Ethane fuel   Oxygen   Carbon Dioxide   Water vapour

(Hydrocarbon)

One of the most popular fossil fuels used on the planet today is coal. Coal burning increased exponentially between 1750 and 1940. This was the period of the first industrial revolution, where steam and electric power were used to mechanise industrial production.

In Britain, coal output rose from about 16 million tonnes in the 1800s to over 200 million tonnes in the 1950s.

Indeed, even in today's world of the 21st century, developing economies still use a huge amount of coal as a source of energy, e.g. China and India.

Other sources of CO_2 emissions are cars and aeroplanes. Emissions from aeroplanes are very damaging because of the height they fly at and of course, petrol and diesel cars are a terrible problem and will be in the foreseeable future.

One study is that *the number of* petrol and diesel *cars worldwide will increase by 2.3 billion between 2005 and 2050, and of these, 1.9 billion will be in emerging and developing countries*[2].

Of all the fossil fuels, coal is the worst… coal should be left in the ground and is by and large, in my opinion the dirtiest fuel available to humanity.

Coal is also another source of unwanted methane, as methane is released once a coal mine is opened.

So, "awful" coal is responsible for carbon dioxide, methane and SO_x being released into the atmosphere.

---

[2] Helm, D. p. 40

Methane and carbon dioxide are produced in the rumen of cattle. Cattle stomachs have four compartments, the rumen, the reticulum, the omasum and the abomasum. When a bullock consumes grass, the grass goes into the first compartment of the stomach, the rumen. This is an anaerobic environment (without oxygen) with a pH between 6.5-7.0 (very slightly acidic to neutral) where bacteria and other microorganisms convert fibre to glucose, with the production of carbon dioxide and methane.

These gases are released through the animal's mouth.

Methane is also released when ice, which has been frozen for thousands of years, melts. This melting, caused by global warming, results in the methane that has been trapped in the ice, being released into the atmosphere. One of the areas of interest is the tundra region of northern Canada and Alaska.

A phenomenon associated with melting ice and less snow at the poles of the earth, is the Albedo effect. As the "white" areas of the planet decrease, the amount of radiation and heat from the sun reflected back into outer space decreases. This is another factor contributing to global warming.

This is the starting point, on our journey towards the formation of a strategy to solve the global warming crisis, which will hopefully result in a sustainable planet.

CHAPTER 2

THE SENTENCE OF LIFE

To devote the attention to the verbs in the sentence of life is to neglect its subject and object

There are an unlimited number of potential projects that interdisciplinary teams of professionals can partake in, to make the world a more sustainable place, by reducing greenhouse gas emissions.

The journey we have embarked on, is a journey towards a sustainable planet. A sustainable planet is one where the balance of nature is preserved, so that future generations can enjoy a clean planet, that is no longer warming up, a planet not polluted by excess greenhouse gases in its atmosphere.

In this chapter, I have decided to look at one project; the construction of a sustainable dwelling house. By sustainable, I mean a dwelling house that sustains life on our planet, in all its wonders. So, sustainability and reducing greenhouse gas emissions, can work as a duo in synchronistic harmony, as we journey to arrest the onset of global warming.

We Think We Own It!

During an election canvass in Ireland, a Green Party candidate at the time announced, that one of their priorities would be to build social houses with easy access to public transport... a good idea, I initially thought. Build houses where the occupants could use public transport instead of petrol cars, therefore reducing their personal carbon footprint (the amount of CO_2 a person's lifestyle is responsible for in one year).

However, after processing the proposal, I ended up questioning it.

My critique was simple... the materials used to build any house will influence global warming, even if the resulting building had easy access to public transport.

Two of the most popular materials used in construction today are huge emitters of CO_2.... Steel and cement.

The manufacture of cement *unfortunately results in a considerable quantity of carbon dioxide emissions*[3].

Virgin general steel has about *three times the carbon footprint of cement*[4].

The four professionals I propose to form this interdisciplinary team are an engineer, a material scientist, a gardener/landscaper and a vet/veterinary technician.

These four professionals must work as a team to produce a "green", "sustainable" dwelling house.

---

[3] Hone, D. p. 101

[4] Berners-Lee, M. p. 101

I shall begin by outlining the difference between a contract and an ecclesiastical (church) covenant.

A contract is an agreement between a boss and an employee, where the employee is subservient to the boss (employer)... an agreement intended to be enforceable by law.

An ecclesiastical covenant on the other hand, is an agreement where all parties have equal influence; no one party is subservient to another and all participants have equal influence... a solemn agreement between the members of a church to act together in harmony with the precepts of the gospel.

For the sake of argument, I propose that the four professionals mentioned have signed an ecclesiastical covenant.

They begin in a positive spirit by adopting the attitude that many opportunities can exist in development works to provide more efficient, lower carbon ways of delivering more improved services (buildings).

Not getting involved in interior design, I have decided to concentrate on the foundations, walls, roof, power supply, water supply, means of heating, light fittings, size, exteriors and the location of this proposed house...

The four continue by agreeing that cement and steel would be used sparingly.

In this first meeting, they with positivity, agree on the following statement... *We have stewardship responsibility – we do not inherit the earth from our ancestors, we bequeath it to our children*[5].

---

[5] Ainger, C. and Fenner, R. p. 5

We Think We Own It!

There you go… echoes of not owning the planet!

Here is what they come up with…

They propose that the foundations should remain a traditional mixture of concrete and steel mesh… then it gets interesting. The walls of this building would be mainly wooden, well insulated, with an outside small brick, using a small amount of mortar, the brick ensuring a nice visual finish.

Since trees are a means of carbon capture and storage, wood is an excellent building material. As a tree grows, through the process of photosynthesis it takes in CO_2 and emits O_2. Once the wood is utilised for building purposes, the CO_2 taken in is stored.

The building design should lead to the situation where minimum energy and minimum water is used in everyday life. This design would mean that the house is efficient and just the correct size for the family/person living there.

The proposed energy sources to heat the building are solar panels, hydroelectric power and wind power. Geothermal heat pumps could also be used, where appropriate.

All light fittings should be environmentally friendly, low energy fittings, e.g. LEDs (light emitting diodes).

A stove that burns logs would be a nice feature on a cold winter's night. To sit in front of it with a good book, would be good for one's soul. Burning wood is part of a closed carbon loop, once trees cut for fuel are replanted.

It is agreed that the building would have an excellent rating within the building rating system.

Now to the roof...

After a well-informed and fair discussion, it is agreed that the traditional slate roof, set at an angle would not be used.

Instead, a green roof is proposed. The idea of a green roof promotes ecosystems, wildlife support and leads to a reduction of rainwater runoff.

Put simply, the roof would be flat... a type of roof garden, where the birds of the air, bees and other wildlife would be most welcome, with rainwater stored and used for toilets and other non-drinkable uses. The veterinary technician/vet and gardener/landscaper had a big say here.

Look at the birds of the air, they neither sow nor reap nor gather into barns, and yet your heavenly Father feeds them[6].

The idea of a vertical garden was also muted, for better air quality and even to grow usable crops.

It was agreed by our four professionals, that most materials used in the building would be reusable and recyclable.

If the house is on the coastline, its location should be on high ground, to allow for the possibility of rising sea levels. An inland house should also be on high ground, to allow for possible future flooding (the unfortunate reality of the world we live in today).

---

[6] Mt. 6:26

Now to the garden or the surrounds of the house… the gardener/ landscaper is let loose. He/she knows what to do and is given due opportunity and respect.

Absolutely no tarmac is proposed… stone driveway, yes… all agree that the ground needs to breathe.

At least one tree should be planted, and if room for a tree is not available, there should be as many green shrubs as possible surrounding the dwelling house.

All costings must be agreed upon and be competitive.

Finally, the house ideally should be located near a public transport system. The green politician finally had his/her say.

CHAPTER 3
WIND ET AL

You cannot paint the wind

Our experiences as we journey to create a more sustainable planet should make us realise that we have to turn away from fossil fuel use, towards renewable, low carbon energy use. However, as this chapter concludes, it will become apparent that inspite of renewable energy research and development, we are far from resolving the problem of global warming.

Low carbon energy sources and renewable energy sources include wind, solar, hydro, nuclear, geothermal, tidal, biomass, algae, hydrogen and batteries (electric vehicles with batteries powered by a renewable energy source).

Now for the critical analysis of each source.

The title of this chapter sums up wind… "you cannot paint the wind". Wind is mysterious, as mysterious as God. *The wind blows where it chooses, and you hear the sound of it, but you do not know where it comes from or where it goes*[7].

---

[7] Jn. 3:8

Wind is free and available in almost all parts of the planet, apart from the doldrums near the equator.

While there are massive positives associated with the use of wind, it has its drawbacks which include the visual intrusion of turbines in sensitive landscapes, noise, bird and bat strikes, and interferences with TV reception, communications and aircraft radar.

Wind as a renewable energy source is expensive to set up; it is intermittent, i.e. wind does not always blow, having a load factor of about 20%; this is the time it generates relative to its maximum potential. Assuming 100% is its maximum potential, this load factor is poor. Because of this poor load factor, wind farms would want to cover a very large area to be an efficient source of power.

Wind farms tend to be located away from areas of large population and they tend to be small-scale at locations remote from demand.

Another potential drawback associated with wind turbines *is that they could lead to surface warming*[8], as they take the kinetic energy from cooling winds on the surface of the planet.

Finally, the manufacture, construction and maintenance of wind turbines is an example of indirect CO_2 e emissions.

Solar, like wind, is freely available to all on the planet, and that is a good thing. However, it too has its drawbacks. The visual intrusion of solar cells in rural and urban environments is not good, while the use of toxic materials such as cadmium, indium and tellurium, have the potential to cause environmental pollution.

---

[8] Hone, D. p. 132

Solar, as a source of renewable energy is very expensive, even more expensive than wind.

On a positive note… *one hour of sunshine is very roughly equal to the world's electricity generation for one year[9].*

So, as a future power source, solar must be an option.

Hydropower has been in operation in Ardnacrusha Ireland on the River Shannon since 1925. While it is CO_2 free, it does create problems. Effects of the construction of dams, effect on rivers and ground water, visual intrusion and risk of accident, downstream effects on agriculture and methane emissions from submerged biomass, are some of the problems associated with hydropower.

Nuclear power is dangerous and to those who attempt to promote nuclear power on the basis that it does not emit CO_2, I suggest they have a rethink. A new nuclear power station embeds a lot of carbon, as it takes a lot of energy to build it. The mining of uranium is another energy-intensive activity. Nuclear energy is therefore, far from CO_2 free.

Geothermal energy can result in the emissions of the polluting gases SO_2 and H_2S combined with the pollution of ground water by chemicals. Heavy metal pollution can also be a problem.

While tidal power is clean and reliable, it can result in the destruction of wildlife habitats and can reduce the dispersion of effluents, which can lead to potential environmental problems.

---

[9] Helm, D. p. 95

Biomass, being a closed carbon loop, sounds good. However, it can have detrimental effects on landscapes, habitats and biodiversity, and it can lead to ground water pollution due to fertilisers used as the crop is grown.

Indeed, energy used in felling trees (biomass), can lead to carbon leakage from a closed carbon loop.

One of the most controversial happenings in the world today is the destruction of rain forests, (the lungs of the earth – as rain forests produce oxygen), to clear land for biomass crops.

Algae, like biomass, is also a closed carbon loop and of course it does not use land. The fact that land is not required (as the algae grows in the ocean), makes algae a better proposition than biofuel/biomass.

Hydrogen is one of the most promising proposed low carbon fuels, with little drawbacks, apart from the cost involved in building the station to separate hydrogen from water using electrolysis. Hydrogen can also be separated from natural gas.

Although hydrogen is a low carbon fuel, it can still potentially cause environmental problems because it emits water vapour when it is burned (H_2O vapour is a greenhouse gas). Therefore, in my opinion, hydrogen is not as environmentally friendly as was initially assumed.

Electric vehicles using a battery will be the future of motoring, *with 2% of cars being electric by 2020*[10]. It is assumed that the electricity

---

[10] Hone, D. p. 203

used to charge these batteries, will be produced using a renewable energy source… perhaps a big assumption.

So unfortunately, sourcing low carbon/renewable energy is not as simple as the sentiment that one "cannot paint the wind".

Reality tells us that there are no carbon free technologies, so it is a question of relative carbon emissions.

Indirect carbon emission (CO_2) is present in all technologies, no matter how environmentally clean they claim to be.

This is surely a sobering thought.

I finish this chapter with a paradox…

CCS (carbon capture and storage), is one of the latest technologies under investigation. When fossil fuel is burned, *the energy emitted is used and the carbon dioxide created is returned back into the ground*[11].

A power station which burns coal and returns the CO_2 produced back into the ground, is the Weyburn project in Saskatchewan, Canada.

The captured CO_2 is pumped to the site of an oil well. Here, the carbon dioxide is pumped into the ground with water, which displaces oil found at great depths.

You might say that CO_2 being used to recover oil, is a CO_2 cycle; however, it is also planned to simply pump CO_2 back into the ground without the displacement of oil, a process called sequestering.

---

[11] Helm, D. p. 207

So, maybe low carbon emission energy is a future possibility, if fossil fuel is burned in conjunction with carbon capture and storage.

A note on the meaning of a "closed carbon loop" and "indirect CO_2 emissions"...

CO_2 can exist in a closed carbon loop, when the CO_2 emitted as a biofuel is burned, is reabsorbed by the cultivation of a new crop of biofuel, (through the process of photosynthesis).

Indirect CO_2 emissions are emissions created by the manufacture and construction of the technology involved in the low carbon/ renewable source of energy being used. An example is the carbon emitted in the manufacture and construction of a wind turbine. I shall explain this term more clearly in the next chapter.

CHAPTER 4

IT HELPS TO KNOW THIS

Sometimes to know where you are going, it helps to know where you have been

We live on a planet that has been slowly heating up since the first industrial revolution of 1750 onwards.

The planet is heating up because of anthropogenic greenhouse gases.

Throughout this book so far, I have mainly used the term CO_2.

I shall use CO_2 e in this chapter... this means carbon dioxide equivalent. It simply means that all greenhouse gases are grouped together under CO_2 e.

Just to recap, I am talking about H_2O, N_2O, CH_4, SO_x and of course CO_2.

I shall also refer to a term called carbon footprint. This is the amount of CO_2 e emitted in any event. It can be emitted directly or indirectly, i.e. CO_2 e emitted behind the scene of an event or process.

Carbon footprint measurement, quantified as tonnes, Kg or ppm (parts per million) CO_2 e, is not a very analytical process. It lacks accuracy and precision. Carbon footprint quantities associated with CO_2 e are referred to as *blurry numbers* in some textbooks[12].

Let us look at the carbon footprint for a banana transported to Ireland from Central America. The banana plant is sown, maintained as it grows, harvested, boxed, transported to an airport, transported by plane and transported by road throughout Ireland. All the direct and indirect CO_2 e emissions throughout its lifetime are approximately quantified. While not being analytical, this blurry number is still a vital piece of data in our battle against global warming. Note that the direct emissions for this banana would be zero, while the indirect emissions are quantified by estimating the actions, associated with production, labour and transport of the banana, already mentioned.

Why is the image of a footprint used? Well, we all know that a foot is made of five toes, metatarsal and heel, (the metatarsal is the base of the foot that touches the ground, between the heel and toes). If one is talking of the footprint of a lifestyle, it is made up of the toes, metatarsal and heel. One toe might be fossil fuel used, another toe might be aeroplane flight, another toe mobile phone use, the metatarsal might be km/year travelled in your petrol car and the heel might be types of fruit eaten for a particular lifestyle.

The carbon footprint of a lifestyle is made up of different activities, just as a foot is made up of different parts, while the carbon footprint for an individual is usually quantified per annum.

---

[12] Berners-Lee, M. p. 5

As previously stated, when calculating CO_2e emissions for the growing and transportation of a banana from Central America to Ireland, they can be termed direct or indirect and the sum of the direct and indirect emissions adds up to the carbon footprint for the activity.

Let us look at another example... the assembly of an electric car. The direct CO_2e emissions for an electric car would calculate to be zero, as it does not produce exhaust fumes.

However, the indirect emissions for this same car would involve the following... emissions due to crude oil processing to make the plastics used, emissions due to the mining of iron ore and the production of the metal used, emissions due to heating and lighting the assembly factory, emissions due to the staff of the factory coming to and going from work... and the list goes on and on.

So, looking at the indirect CO_2e emissions, the carbon footprint for a new electric car is enormous... something not mentioned by the manufacturers.

Now, let us look at a number of different carbon footprints for different life scenarios.

All text messages sent and received from all mobile phones worldwide in a year calculates as *32,000 tonnes CO_2e*[13].

A banana, (already discussed), arriving in Ireland from Central America calculates as *80 g CO_2e*[14].

---

[13] Ibid, p. 11

[14] Ibid, p. 27

We live in a world of high-powered smart-phones. Global mobile phone usage for a year calculates as *125 million tonnes $CO_2 e$*[15].

Walking through a doorway in various weather conditions results in some very interesting data...

During summer, on a warm day, walking through a doorway calculates as *zero $CO_2 e$*. Walking through a normal dwelling house door on a cold winter's day calculates as *3 g $CO_2 e$,* while walking through a large store's automatic electric doors on a cold winter's day calculates as *84 g $CO_2 e$*[16].

Now to the troubling scenario... walking through an opened high street store entrance on a cold winter's day. This involves a shocking amount of $CO_2 e$ emissions, not mentioned/calculated in the reference book I used for this section... the problem being that the store is being heated as the entrance door remains open. Finally, in a previous chapter, I mentioned the renewable energy source that is a wind turbine. While it does not emit any $CO_2 e$, the construction of one turbine emits *30 tonnes $CO_2 e$* (indirect $CO_2 e$ emissions)[17].

So, what can humanity do to counteract global warming, using the examples I used in this chapter?

It is a healthy pastime eating fruit and bananas; however, when you buy a banana or any fruit, make sure to eat it and not throw it in a bin.

---

[15] Ibid, p. 113

[16] Ibid, p. 14

[17] Ibid, p. 146

I would say the jury is still out on purchasing a new electric car. Maybe one is better off keeping one's petrol banger for the time being!

In my opinion, we should reduce our use of smart-phones and i-phones, and where possible, we might be better off using a small Nokia phone instead. If this is not an option, the use of phones should be reduced and only used for text messages and phone messages... try to reduce your time spent on social media, virtual reality pastimes, WhatsApp, YouTube, Facebook, TikTok, Twitter, games and other mobile phone apps.

To all store owners... I know having a door open in all weather conditions promotes business, but why not keep the door closed, or perhaps use an electric door that automatically opens and closes when needed, and have a clear sign signifying that you are...

"Sustainably aware and open for business".

Finally, looking at the indirect CO_2 e emissions estimated for the construction of a wind turbine, perhaps the world should have a rethink regarding the widespread use of wind as a renewable source of energy.

Looking at the hills around Cappawhite and Glengar in Co. Tipperary, Ireland, it might be too late, as the once scenic view is not as scenic anymore, due to the many wind turbines that have appeared over the past five years or so.

While we know where we have been and where we are at this moment in time, we can still look to the future with hope in our hearts. However, as we step into the future, we must learn to live our lives more sustainably by emitting less CO_2e both directly and indirectly. This target can be achieved if we decide to change our attitude and lifestyle, where energy conservation will be on our minds and in our hearts, and will become central to the way we live our lives.

Put simply, if we use less energy in our daily lives, we will reduce the amount of CO_2e emissions we are responsible for, which will result in a reduction in our own personal carbon footprint.

CHAPTER 5

THE PROBLEM WITH THE SNAKE

A good place for snakes, if there is such a thing, is a good place

I mentioned in my abstract, that (in my opinion) global warming has been and still is fanned by humanity's ability to mislead others, in its selfish desire for property and wealth.

Now, as I begin this chapter, I soften my attitude, by inserting the pronoun "some".

"Some" of humanity mislead others in their selfish desire for property and wealth.

That sounds less harsh, yet the problem still exists... and this problem of "some" fans global warming.

Where did this darkness originate? Is it a result of a possible destructive gene in our DNA or is there another explanation?

I am no geneticist; however, in my reading on the subject, I have discovered that genetics does suggest a lying gene. A strong genetic component known as pseudologia fantastica can lead a person to partake in chronic outrageous lies.

I shall now stick to something I am more comfortable with… I shall concentrate on theology, philosophy and mythology as I attempt to trace this darkness by dipping into a story written many years ago. The story I speak of, is the creation story of the Bible found in the Book of Genesis. But before I proceed, I want to acknowledge other traditions and how they tell stories of how the world began. The splitting in two of a cosmic egg originating in China, a void when all was darkness spoken about by the Hebrews… everything beginning in chaos (the Greeks)… Egypt and Mesopotamia setting the scene with boundless ocean… the people of India telling stories based on Hindu traditions, while the Japanese tell a story of creation, which leads not so much to the first man, but to the first Emperor.

As I wear my theological/philosophical/mythological hat, I shall now refer to the Bible, the book of Genesis and the story of Adam and Eve in the Garden of Eden. Did Adam and Eve ever exist, or is this a mythological story from ancient times, written in order to attempt to understand the origins of the depths of human nature, warts and all?

I feel it is mythological, but it still contains vitally important theology too.

To begin with, creation was very good… *God saw everything he had made, and indeed, it was very good*[18].

All was going well, until Satan, in the form of a serpent, appeared.

---

[18] Gen. 1:31

Up to that moment in time, Adam and Eve were living in harmony with the earth and nature. They had access to everything, except the tree of the knowledge of good and evil, and its fruit.

God had instructed them to avoid this area of the garden... *You shall not eat of the fruit of the tree that is in the middle of the garden, nor shall you touch it, or you shall die*[19].

They were happy to follow God's wishes, as they lived in blissful happiness, in harmony with the planet, each other and the natural world. They possessed the gift of contentment, being content with their state of existence; at that moment in the continuum that is space and time.

Eve however, was innocent, pure and naive... never having experienced anybody/anything that could/would mislead her.

The cunning dark evil serpent, Satan, noticed her childish/pure innocence and got inside her head and heart. "It" manipulated her and misled her into thinking that it would be a harmless action, if she picked the fruit from the tree of the knowledge of good and evil, and ate it.

"It" went so far as to say that she would not die, and she would become like God if she ate the fruit!

But the serpent said to the woman, *you will not die, for God knows when you eat it your eyes will be opened, and you will be like God, knowing good and evil*[20].

---

[19] Gen. 3:3

[20] Ibid, 3:4-5

The serpent misled Eve. She picked the fruit, ate it and gave it to Adam, he ate it and the rest is history... a history that continues today as the Amazon rain forest burns[21].

As Adam and Eve walked out through the east gate of the Garden of Eden, a cherubim was placed there with a flaming sword.

This was the mythological beginning of CO_2 e emissions... emissions that continue today.

Christian theology associates Original Sin with the taking of this forbidden fruit... Adam and Eve's sin which is believed to be passed onto us.

I read a very interesting book called *Crossing Reclaiming the Landscape of Our Lives,* by Mark Barrett, O.S.B., a Benedictine priest, a number of years ago, and it looked at this moment, which led to the concept of Original Sin, in a broader, more enlightened way.

Mark, writing about this moment in time, referring to the *medieval author of the Theologia Germanica*, is of the opinion that Adam's fall did not happen because he ate the apple, his fall happened *because of his claiming something for his own. Had he eaten seven apples, and yet never claimed anything for his own, he would not have fallen: but as soon as he called something his own, he fell and would have fallen if he had never touched an apple*[22].

As Adam proudly looked around the garden and landscape of Eden in all its splendour, with the apple (fruit) in his hand, believing that

---

[21] The summer of 2019

[22] Barrett, M. p. 112

he owned all he saw and held, the seed responsible for humanity's selfish desire for property and wealth was first sown, and still flourishes today in the 21st Century.

Adam failed to open his stony heart at that moment in time, he failed to appreciate and embrace the beautiful gift of creation present before his eyes... he was afraid of what Mark Barrett refers to as the river of change.

He attempted to *control* what was *unpredictable and unpossessable*[23], as his only desire was to own it.

He thought/imagined at that moment that he owned what he saw and held, ignoring the Omnipotent God of creation, a creation that is ever changing, mysterious and dynamic.

I am reminded of Heraclitus' saying about the river of change over 2,600 years ago... *It is not possible to step into the same river twice*[24].

The river changes and the person stepping into the river changes, both the person and the river are unpredictable and unpossessable. Adam failed to see this, and as a result sowed the seed present in the hearts of some of humanity... resulting in the self-destructive, crippling desire for property and wealth.

As a result of this seed sown by our mythological parents, humanity's hardness of heart fans a selfish desire to own things... including the planet.

---

[23] Barrett, M. p. 111

[24] Magee, B. p. 14

The serpent (Satan) planted the seed of the dark art of misleading a person or nation, while Adam, because of his hardness of heart, combined with not recognising the fact that creation is dynamic and always changing, planted the seed for humanity's selfish desire for property and wealth.

The effects of both these seeds are seen in certain areas of our world today and in my opinion fan global warming.

I have assumed that the snake/serpent is Satan… The New St Jerome Biblical Commentary does not quite agree… stating that the snake is not Satan; however, it also states that later traditions interpret "it" as Satan.

The Book of Wisdom clearly states that the serpent was Satan. *But through the devil's envy death entered the world, and those who belong to his company experience it*[25].

Matthew Henry's concise Biblical commentary clearly states… *Satan assaulted our first parents… the tempter was the devil… the devil was from the beginning a murderer and the great mischief maker… he is a liar… it is the craft of Satan to speak of the Divine Law as uncertain or unreasonable… Satan teaches first to doubt and then to deny… he aims to make all discontent with their present state… thus let us resist the devil, and he will flee from us*[26].

The Exultet, a hymn of Easter Saturday night sung by a Deacon, has an interesting slant on the happening I have recalled. The Exultet refers to this moment as a *Happy Fault*[27], or "Felix Culpa".

---

[25] Wis. 2:24

[26] www.christianity.com/bible/commentary/matthew-henry-concise/genesis/3

[27] CCC. p. 93

What is happy about this, one might ask?

It is seen as a happy event, as it opened the way for Jesus Christ to be born into humanity as Messiah and Saviour, where His crucifixion and death on a cross led to the Resurrection.

This story of salvation is the reason Pope Francis lives in the Vatican today, next to the holy relic of the Throne of Peter.

Genesis is therefore much more than a story of mythology...

In my opinion, the following happenings are the signs of humanity's failings/weaknesses in the world today, sown in Eden, which fan global warming.

We are not content to holiday at home; we have an obsession with globe-trotting, looking to experience the ultimate holiday experience, as CO_2 e emissions from aeroplanes are continuously dumped into the atmosphere.

We are not living in harmony with nature, sometimes we are the enemy of nature... deforestation of the world's rain forests is one glaring example.

Assault happens in various forms… physical assault and character assault being two of the commonest examples.

Violence and murder are growing problems within humanity, and the murder of eco systems and nature's balance is continuously happening before our eyes.

Taking part in mischief… just look at the political set up globally... making money for economies at the cost of nature's beauty and balance. The political discussions regarding global warming have drawn a blank... nothing but empty promises. The Irish political parties negotiating a Coalition Parliament (summer 2020) proposed an annual decrease in CO_2e emissions of 7%. All talk at the time of writing. The scandal of Ireland buying itself out of meeting its emission targets is one of the unspoken scandals hidden by our politicians. Up to 2019, Ireland had spent approximately 121 million Euro buying carbon credits.

Crafty lies... Politics and even Church are in my opinion guilty parties when it comes to the telling of lies. One could even refer to the politics of church!

Some of us doubt the existence of God; more absolutely deny the existence of God, while others use the name of God to sell newspapers... *OMI GOD*[28].

In Ireland of the 21st Century, what was once the common saying in times of tragedy... "our thoughts and prayers are with the family", has been replaced by some with... "our thoughts are with the family"...while "Thank God" has been replaced with "Thank Goodness".

Finally, our desire for property and wealth is destroying the planet. As the Amazon rain forest burned during the summer of 2019, the Brazilian president tackled the problem internally, without seeking aid from other countries. He must have been convinced that it was Brazil's property[29]... and Brazil's property alone... "The lungs of the earth".

---

[28] Phelan, C. p. 1

[29] www.irishtimes.com/news/world/amazon-fires-brazilian-states-ask-for-military-help-amid-record-blazes-1.3996476

Finally, if there is such a thing as a good place for the snake of Eden, it is surely Hell.

CHAPTER 6

THE HELPFUL OCEAN

Nothing happens quickly
in deep water

We live on a planet where 70% of the surface is water. As anthropogenic greenhouse gases are emitted, some of the gases go into the atmosphere and some into the oceans. As CO_2 is constantly moving from the atmosphere into the ocean, eventually an equilibrium of CO_2 concentration will be set up between these two mediums. This equilibrium is not yet fixed, as there is a lag or hysteresis between the ability of the ocean and the atmosphere to absorb CO_2 and of course CO_2 levels are still rising in the atmosphere.

Overall, our oceans have absorbed up to 30% of anthropogenic greenhouse gases over the past 300 years.

This has greatly helped our situation.

Some of the absorbed CO_2 is converted back into oxygen, through the process of photosynthesis involving plant-like organisms called phytoplankton.

CO_2 is released out of the ocean as it warms up, and conversely, CO_2 is absorbed back into the ocean, as it cools.

Ocean water cools down and heats up, as it travels around the globe in the various ocean currents, so the relationship between CO_2 concentration in the atmosphere and the ocean is constantly changing and is very much a dynamic process.

However, what is not dynamic is the fact that the amount of anthropogenic CO_2 greenhouse gas produced is still rising. This is the persistent concern running throughout this book.

One of the major problems with increased levels of CO_2 in our oceans is the production of carbonic acid.

$$H_2O \quad + \quad CO_2 \quad \rightarrow \quad H_2CO_3$$

Ocean water   Carbon dioxide   Carbonic acid

CO_2 dissolved in seawater reacts with it to produce carbonic acid. This carbonic acid increases ocean acidity, which in turn leads to the death of the coral reefs around the world.

The combination of rising temperatures and rising acid levels in our oceans, is destroying this jewel of the natural world.

The fact that the ocean has absorbed up to 30% of greenhouse gases produced, has been a good thing. The ocean is a natural sink for carbon dioxide... and of course it will continue to absorb carbon dioxide from the atmosphere, if emissions ever reduce.

However, the constant rise in the temperature and acidity of the ocean is not good and is a worrying issue for the planet. This is a very slow process, yet a deadly one...

CHAPTER 7

WORDS

If you have the words,
you will always find a way

The politics of global warming has involved lots of words and some action, but unfortunately has not caused any reduction in anthropogenic greenhouse gas emissions.

Mixed with politics is economics. The following questions are sometimes asked... are measures to counteract global warming profitable?... and do they create jobs?

Unfortunately, measures to counteract global warming do not by and large, add to the wealth of any economy.

So, as politicians and economists continue to talk and plan, greenhouse gas emissions continue to spiral out of control.

This is tragic and shocking.

The stark reality is that we inhabit an ill planet. A symptom of this illness is an atmospheric temperature rise, and this illness has been diagnosed as global warming.

We Think We Own It!

This planet is on the verge of needing intensive care. It needs rest... rest in the form of a major reduction in anthropogenic greenhouse gas emissions, and the only way it can attain this rest is through our actions.

Scientists, by studying ancient air bubbles trapped in ice, have been able to measure CO_2 levels in the atmosphere over the past 400,000 years.

This study has shown CO_2 levels to be higher today, than at any time during this 400,000-year period, and they are still rising[30].

The politicians began talking back in 1997 in Kyoto, Japan.

As 2012 arrived, it was obvious to all that the initial goals formulated in Kyoto were not going to be achieved.

The political talk has continued, with the latest agreement signed on global warming being the Paris agreement (2016). Most *UNFCCC* (United Nations Framework Convention on Climate Change) countries have signed up.

The focus of this agreement is to keep the global rise in temperature below 2° C, from pre-industrial revolution times.

Since the initial Kyoto agreement back in 1997, politicians have played quite a game.

Democratic nations have mingled with Communist nations, while the political/economic strategy of making as much money as possible, has continuously hovered in the background.

---

[30] www.scrippsco2.ucsd.edu/history_legacy/keeling_curve_lessons.html

In the twenty-three years between 1997 and 2020, the planet has got hotter, greenhouse gas emissions have continued to increase at an alarming rate, and there still hasn't been a universal plan to tackle these tragic developments.

Corruption between nations and politicians has been rife, struggles between Democracies and Communist countries have been ongoing... Some countries have shown little real interest, while the USA is threatening to pull out of the Paris agreement altogether... (summer 2020).

Interest in climate change appears to be a luxury good - fine when economies are doing well (as long as it does not cost too much), but not so pressing otherwise.[31]

Canada and Russia are gaining economically, as they tap oil and gas reserves due to melting ice. The recession in Europe during 2009 meant that ordinary people were no longer interested in climate change, because they struggled for money and jobs.

One of the outcomes of the Paris agreement was that each country promised to create a home-grown plan to tackle climate change.

Ireland has proposed an ambitious plan.

180 different measures have been proposed to reduce greenhouse gas emissions... it is hoped to have NET zero emissions by 2050... (this simply means that when emissions are measured against our ability to store carbon, or take it out of the atmosphere, the balance will be zero).

---

[31] Helm, D. p. 165

The proposed measures include... increasing carbon taxes, retro fitting houses to make them more economical to heat, promoting electric vehicles, changing how we produce energy with an emphasis on renewable energy, reducing emissions from agriculture (it is responsible for 33% of emissions presently) and finally planting more trees.

It is planned to maintain economic growth as these measures are implemented.

This bold plan has now been set in stone in the form of an amended Bill, (March 2021).

The Climate Action Bill published yesterday is the most ambitious legislation of its type in any country yet, the Government has said, as it plans to enshrine in law a target to halve carbon emissions by 2030 and to achieve net-zero emissions by 2050[32].

Having read this amended Bill, I am sorry to say, that in my opinion, it is an example of more political words.

These words include a proposed 51% reduction in CO_2 e emissions by 2030 and the creation of a Climate Neutral Economy by 2050. This is defined as a *sustainable economy and society, where greenhouse gas emissions are balanced or exceeded by the removal of greenhouse gas*[33].

In other words, we plan to continue emitting CO_2 e, while we may plant more trees or find other ways of removing it from the atmosphere... or we might end up buying more carbon credits.

---

[32] O'Sullivan, K. and McGee, H. p. 1

[33] Climate action and low carbon (amendment) Bill, Government of Ireland, 2021

In the event that the planned policies and measures contained in the Climate Action Plan (March 2021), are insufficient to meet Ireland's annual targets... Ireland may need to purchase additional credits during the 2021-2030 period[34].

I am astonished that our politicians still continue to (in my opinion) mislead the Irish people, by putting together such an unsustainable plan for our future.

As far as I am concerned, this amended Bill changes nothing... it is simply more words... words... and words...

Now, what is this about "buying carbon credits"?

The Kyoto agreement created a new commodity called "carbon". Countries started trading in carbon, to help them achieve their emission targets. Countries that had emission units to spare (emission units permitted to them, but not used) could sell their excess carbon capacity to countries whose emissions were over their agreed limit. Up to 2019, Ireland has spent up to 121 million Euro buying itself out of failed International Environmental targets, for carbon emissions agreed in Kyoto, by purchasing the right to pollute from countries that polluted less.

A member of the Irish Parliament has said, (June 2019), it was "horrific" that Irish taxpayers' money had been spent by the NTMA purchasing carbon credits from other European countries, in order to meet its targets.

---

[34]www.irishtimes.com/news/ireland/irish-news/government-is-warned-of-high-cost-of-not-achieving-climate-action-plan-1.4035349

He continued... *essentially Ireland is pretending it can meet its targets*[35].

Companies can also partake in this charade.

They can claim to be carbon emission free or carbon neutral, by purchasing carbon credits from organisations that can create carbon credits, this is also termed *carbon offsetting*[36]. These organisations may be involved in afforestation or similar enterprises that store carbon.

Humanity's ability to mislead, a seed sown in Eden many years ago, once again raises its head.

I finish with two depressing, sobering thoughts... A sentiment shared in a book I read, published a number of years ago, and a radio discussion I heard during spring 2021.

The book quotation goes as follows...

By carrying out a largely fruitless process for years (Political discussion on climate change), *pretending progress is being made, the need to explore alternatives is not given the priority it deserves*[37].

The discussion on RTE radio 1 went as follows...

A politician was asked a straight question... *you promised a 7% reduction on carbon emissions last year, did you as a Government achieve this target?*

---

[35] www.thejournal.ie/ireland-carbon-credits-emissions-4901302-Nov2019/

[36] www.britannica.com/technology/carbon-offset

[37] Helm, D. p. 165

The response was disappointing, but unfortunately, not unexpected.

The politician spoke about planning for the future, various committee meetings happening at a Government level and money being invested in renewable energy sources. He concluded by saying that he was hopeful of new jobs being created in the whole area of renewable energy production, which will replace the jobs lost in the area of energy production involving fossil fuels.

He went on and on and on, but didn't answer the question asked...

Did you as a government achieve the target of a 7% reduction in CO_2 e emissions in the past year[38]?

I now propose a different strategy, away from the world of politics and economics... because in my opinion, words will still play a part, but we shall also need the right actions, attitude and thinking.

---

[38] RTE radio discussion program, 2021

CHAPTER 8

THE THIRD WORLD MATTERS

No person has the right to fix the boundary to the march of a man. No person has the right to say to another man – thus far shalt thou go and no further
(Charles Stuart Parnell)

In the preceding chapters, I have discussed global warming from the point of view of the First and Second Worlds.

There is another section of the world population (whom I consider the forgotten) who also call this planet home… those of the Third World.

Do the inhabitants of the Third World, the bottom billion people – those attempting to survive on no more than a dollar a day, have a say in this debate?

Does the drive for low carbon energy sources, or alternative renewable energy sources, make any difference to this section of the world's population… those people who never owned a refrigerator, a car, a computer or took a plane journey?

If we, in the First and Second Worlds foolishly think that we own the planet, what about the bottom billion people... do they own anything... do they think they own anything?

Personally, I know they do not own a lot. They can barely feed themselves, never mind harbour thoughts of owning the planet.

So, what role, if any, have these people in the fight against global warming... and more importantly, have we the right to fix the boundaries of potential life learnings and experiences for these economically disadvantaged people? Just because of the mess we have created by over-using the planet's resources, have we the right to instruct these people to reduce their carbon footprint, when it is tiny anyway?

Can we order them to live more sustainably, when they are barely living or even surviving?

It is a fact that emissions per head of the population are much lower in developing countries – because they have less income per head, and even lower in Third World countries, because they hardly have an income.

Our world is so consumeristic, that a new term must be introduced along with carbon emission and that is carbon consumption. Carbon consumption is a major problem for the First and Second Worlds today.

I return to the example mentioned in chapter 4, the example of a brand-new electric car, with zero direct CO_2 emissions. The carbon consumed in the manufacture/assembly of that new electric car, is termed indirect CO_2 emission or carbon consumption.

When we purchase a brand-new electric car, we can boast about the car having zero direct emissions of CO_2; however, we consume CO_2 when the car is purchased by us, as CO_2 is emitted as the car is assembled.

An ongoing problem with the First and Second Worlds is the reality of Jevons' paradox. It is a proven fact that as energy efficiency improves and energy gets cheaper... more energy is consumed. The invention of the LED (light emitting diode), was a major breakthrough in energy efficient light bulbs. What happened next? More and more LEDs were introduced into private houses and businesses...

Just imagine all the Christmas trees around the globe, all using LED lights... whatever was gained with the invention of the LED has been lost by the reality of an over consumption of energy by humanity.

Will humanity ever stop and think? Or do we have a self-destructive gene?

Unlike any other creature that lived before, we have become a geophysical force, *swiftly changing the atmosphere and climate, as well as the composition of the world's fauna and flora*[39].

In my opinion, humanity is being misled by the misleading story being continuously spun by world politicians, *that the energy sector can be converted from an overwhelmingly carbon-based one to almost zero carbon in half a century*[40].

---

[39] Helm, D. p. 237
[40] Ibid, p. 238

The unfortunate influence of the serpent of Eden is alive and well in today's world!

A mathematical formula (model) called the Kaya identity developed by Japanese energy economist Yoichi Kaya bases the future of energy production and greenhouse gas emissions for the planet, on the following parameters: efficiency, energy source, population and development (wealth).

Analysis carried out over a twenty-year period (1990 – 2011), led by Professor Azadeh Tavakoli (Iran) using this model, produced very positive results regarding its precision and accuracy[41].

However, David Hone claims that in most analyses using this same model, *population* and *development* have been ignored. The fact that *population* and *development* (wealth) are increasing (and being ignored), suggests (according to Hone) that this mathematical model is possibly misleading the world, by underestimating projected greenhouse gas emissions[42].

This difference in opinion regarding the precision and accuracy of the Yoichi Kaya mathematical model, predicting possible greenhouse gas emissions, once again has the "fingerprint" (if snakes had fingers) of the misleading serpent of Eden.

Our present strategy uses this thinking, so in my opinion we need to find a different strategy.

---

[41] Tavakoli, A.

[42] Hone, D. p. 60

This brings me back to the Third World and India in particular. *In 2016, only about one in four of the country's* (India's) *homes contained a fridge. That compares to an average of 99% of households in developed countries*[43].

Nobody is talking about the Third World in this debate on global warming... *Several billion people still aspire to a first refrigerator, a first car or perhaps a long-haul flight to visit other parts of the world*[44].

The people who occupy this beautiful planet represent the First, Second and Third Worlds, and all have equal rights.

This makes the problem, and possible solution, to this global warming crisis most complicated, and a lot more complex than the world's politicians are allowing us to see.

Thank God, the Third World countries are slowly developing... and these people are entitled to develop, own a refrigerator, a car, a computer and take a journey on an aeroplane.

We in the developed world, have no right to stop their march or development.

The solution to this problem is not as simple as Governments spending taxpayers' money on renewable energy, insulating houses, expanding public transport, introducing carbon taxes and eliminating the use of fossil fuels, along with other suggestions put forward by world leaders and politicians.

---

[43] Hone, D. p. 192

[44] Ibid, p. 237

We must change our attitudes and think of others. We must refrain from fixing boundaries and stopping marches, especially when it comes to the poor of the Third World.

CHAPTER 9

KINDNESS AND CHANGE

One act of random kindness at a time changes the world

I quote Morgan Scott Peck... *discipline is the basic set of tools we require to solve life's problems*[45].

We have a problem... global warming... and there is no easy solution; it will take discipline and it will involve pain to attempt to address it.

Confronted with the reality of World War II, *Winston Churchill informed British civilians that he offered nothing but, blood, toil, tears and sweat.* The public engaged... curtailed their lifestyles and supported the cause[46].

We have a world problem... and I believe one of the important things we must do is cut back on our carbon (energy) consumption... in other words, we must *crunch*[47] our carbon consumption.

---

[45] Peck, M., S. p. 13

[46] Helm, D. p. 242

[47] Ibid.

We need to lower our standards of living globally and reduce the amount of energy we use.

We need to reduce our personal carbon footprint.

We will need discipline to do this, and we will have to endure pain.

There is simply no easy solution to this global warming crisis, and it will not be solved by political talk and proposals, or by money alone...

Granted, great things are happening in the area of renewable energy and scientific research and development, however, in my opinion, contemplating a new direction will prove fruitful.

Focus up to now has been to maintain and possibly increase the amount of energy we produce and consume, while moving away from fossil fuels, towards low carbon energy sources and renewable energy sources.

In my opinion, something else needs to happen...

Science is instructing us to *reduce global emissions of CO_2 e by 50% by 2050* to stop a global temperature rise of 2° C above pre-industrial times[48].

We are looking at one of the biggest elephant in the room scenarios[49] ever. We seem determined to reduce CO_2 e emissions by 50%, yet we plan to maintain energy consumption/production at present rates with a possible eye towards increasing it... this in my opinion, is a totally unsustainable outlook.

---

[48] Everett, B., Boyle, G., Peake, S., and Ramage, J. p. 612

[49] Stoanes, C., Stevenson, A. p. 462

Then we have the situation with our Third World neighbours. We need to send some energy their way, for them to own their first refrigerator, car, computer and take their first excursion on an aeroplane. They are entitled to experience this aspect and gift life has to offer.

Our current plan moving forward (promoted by World Governments) to tackle the global warming crisis is to encourage energy efficiency, fuel switching, carbon capture and storage, and the use of renewable energy sources.

There has been no solid proposal put forward by World Governments encouraging humanity to change their lifestyles (change their behaviour) and reduce their personal carbon footprint, by reducing the amount of energy they consume.

The conclusion I come to, after careful reading and research, is that we need to change our lifestyles, we need to change our behaviour... and we need to reduce our personal carbon footprint.

How can we do this... how can we change our lifestyle and reduce our own personal carbon footprint... which may well result in a reduction in our personal standard of living?

One act of human kindness at a time can change the world and can counteract the crisis we find ourselves in.

It will take a certain amount of self-sacrifice (or pain), a certain amount of human kindness and a change in behaviour. Having reflected on all this, I have arrived at the following suggestions...

Reduce air travel… do we really need to travel to a foreign country for our summer vacation every year? Perhaps we should ground all airlines worldwide one day a week.

Insist on energy efficient light fittings everywhere, e.g. LEDs (light emitting diodes).

Create walkable cities, where it is not necessary to use a car to reach shops or schools.

We need to retro fit/insulate our homes and reduce the amount of energy needed to heat them.

When heating a house in wintertime, heat the one room you are spending most of the day in.

Similarly, only have substantial lighting switched on in the room you are occupying, late at night.

We need to eliminate the use of wide-open doorways to department stores on cold winter days. In my opinion, it would be better to replace them with electric doors that open and close as customers come and go.

When designing new houses and housing estates, we should move towards a more sustainable design, discussed in chapter 2 and a smaller design… and of course any new dwelling house should be built near public transport. For any World Government, I would strongly suggest environmental policies and housing policies should be interconnected.

We need to work more from home… do we really need to travel to work every day?

We should cycle more.

Trains should be used more… journeys between cities within a continent should be taken by inter-city trains rather than by air, because train travel causes less pollution than air travel. Of course, the infrastructure would need to be built, which would create CO_2 emissions; however, long term, this would be a good policy.

Seldom drive a one-person car where possible… When using a car, the car should be full… car-pooling should be more popular. We should move away from one car/one person scenarios, (this was pre-Covid-19 thinking).

We need to eliminate Jevons' Paradox or the so called rebound effect. If we purchase a more sustainable car, we should refrain from driving it more… if we save money on heating by insulating our home, we should not spend the money saved on an energy-intensive flight to a far off holiday destination.

I suggest that we should get into the habit of tossing a coin if we are trying to decide on doing something which might use excess energy... heads you do it, tails you wait for another day. Over a few years, on the law of averages, this should reduce one's energy consumption.

I have recently heard advertisements for electric toothbrushes on Irish radio, (Summer 2021)... what a waste of energy. Between wasting precious energy and indirect CO_2 emissions associated with the manufacture of these toothbrushes, this has to be one of the most unsustainable products ever to be put on a shelf of a retail store.

We must look at our use of technology and ask the difficult question… do we really need to carry around such a powerful device in our pockets or hand/shoulder bags, to keep in touch with work colleagues, friends and family? Do we really need to take a photo of an ice cream we are about to bite into… or a photo of a freshly cooked stew? Do we really need to take all those selfies? I say, reduce time spent on fancy i-phones and smart-phones, use them sparingly or even decide on using a simple Nokia phone for text messages and phone calls. This is some of the pain I have mentioned. On the subject of Facebook, Twitter, TikTok,WhatsApp, etc., I feel we should reduce our time spent on these social media platforms. We need to spend less time in a virtual world and more time in reality. A statement I once heard on Irish radio (Ryan Tubridy) really summed up social media/technology and its influence on Democracy… *Democracy swims and dies in technology*[50]. I am aware that this type of thinking will be particularly difficult on the generation that has grown up with technology. Yet, I feel a reduction in the use of some technology is something that must be contemplated by all generations.

On the topic of new electric cars… I am going to astound you now, but I believe it is more environmentally friendly to keep driving your old petrol car. The amount of indirect carbon emitted during the manufacturing process of a new electric car is colossal. Old cars should remain on the road for a longer lifetime than we are currently allowing.

Now, I return to Eden and the encounter with the serpent (Satan) who misled our first parents. We need to address these theological/ mythological happenings. I feel we need to change our attitude towards life and refrain from the tendency to mislead others, in our quest for wealth and property. We need to open our hearts and

---

[50] RTE Radio 1 Ireland, Ryan Tubridy Show

realise that this planet is not owned by us. This is easily the most challenging suggestion I have made so far.

Continuing with Eden... we should aim to plant at least one tree in our lifetime, which is an example of natural CCS (carbon capture and storage). Land use can change in some parts of Ireland and the world, where planting trees would be seen and accepted as a viable use for agricultural land. By planting more trees, the amazing rain forests could be carefully maintained and repaired where needed, by replanting trees that have been felled or have been destroyed by fire.

During the Christmas season, billions of natural Christmas trees are cut down worldwide, as the use of artificial trees are now being discouraged. However if you do have an artificial tree, which you purchased a few years ago, don't dispose of it... keep using it, because as the years go by, it is in a way recuperating the CO_2 emissions it originally emitted during its manufacture.

Continuing on the topic of Christmas... on November the 10th, 2021 the Christmas lights were turned on in Dublin City. In my opinion, THIS SHOULD NEVER HAPPEN AGAIN. If we are serious about reducing CO_2 emissions, we should wait until nearer to the season of Christmas, to turn on Christmas lights. I feel December 21st each year would be an appropriate moment. At this moment humanity could join in mutual love, respect and harmony[51] with our ancestors of 3,300 BC when they marked this moment. An example of one of these places of pre-Christian ritual can be found in Newgrange

---

[51] Gen. 2:25

Ireland... a monument *built in precise alignment with the rising sun over the solstice each winter* in the Northern Hemisphere[52].

We, (the people of Ireland), have the greatest grasslands in the world for dairy cattle and dry cattle. These dumb animals produce methane and carbon dioxide, through the miracle of their digestive systems, as they digest grass. We as a country are a world leader in beef and milk production... I personally would not touch this industry.

Continuing with the topic of food... any food (or fruit) purchased, should be consumed and not dumped as refuse.

In my opinion, carbon tax is not necessary... instead governments should simply encourage people to use less fossil fuels.

I believe coal burning should be banned straight away. Opening coalmines causes methane to be released... while burning coal emits carbon dioxide and other toxic gases such as oxides of sulphur, oxides of nitrogen and carbon monoxide. Coal is one of the most toxic, unhealthy substances on this planet. Waste produced by coal burning power stations (fly ash) carries into the surrounding environment a hundred times more radiation than a nuclear power station producing the same amount of energy.

Smokeless coal, while being cleaner than natural coal, is still a problem. In a study carried out by University College Dublin, it was found that fuels categorised as 'smokeless' under Irish law, were found to generate very substantial levels of particulate emissions. So, smokeless coal burning should also be banned.

---

[52] www.newgrange.com/winter_solstice.htm

Staying on the topic of energy production, all low carbon renewable energy sources should be encouraged, while more R&D (research and development) on the whole area should be financed and encouraged.

Do not be so hasty to throw away your old clothes, donate them to a second-hand shop and perhaps get into the habit of buying good quality second-hand clothes yourself.

Do not drink plastic bottled water, drink tap water.

Do not leave a radio and lights switched on at home when you are away.

Saint Patrick's Day is a huge celebration for Irish people worldwide. It is celebrated on the 17th of March every year. In recent years, an increasingly popular trend has been to light up major buildings and important sites around the world with green lighting for the day. I feel this should simply stop straight away, to reduce energy consumption.

I believe we need to travel less, sit more, relax and simply be. We need to enjoy our beautiful home and the beauty that nature has to offer. We need to become more silent and we need to listen, listen to ourselves, listen to others, listen to *nature*[53], listen to the bird call every morning and evening; we need to become more aware of the mystery of our origins on this planet through the stories of theology, philosophy and mythology... and finally we need to get into the habit of acting with kindness, being nice to each other and simply looking out for each other. In addition we need to reduce our

---

[53] Wright, I. p. 49

use of energy, technology and distractive noise, and find more time to stand and stare…

What is this life if, full of care,
We have no time to stand and stare?

No time to stand beneath the boughs,
And stare as long as sheep or cows.

No time to see, when woods we pass,
Where squirrels hid their nuts in grass.

No time to see, in broad daylight,
Streams full of stars, like stars at night:

No time to turn at beauty's glance,
And watch her feet, how they can dance:

No time to wait till her mouth can
Enrich that smile her eyes began?

A poor life this, if full of care,
We have no time to stand and stare[54].

All these suggestions I have made, brings me back to what I mentioned earlier in this book; a possible new strategy is needed, a new plan, a new approach.

---

[54] Walsh, T.F. p. 66. (Davies, W.H.)

I feel we need to seriously look at a new strategy to counteract the onset of global warming, as the strategy used up to now, which has been driven by politics, science and economics, in a world influenced by the ability of some, to mislead others in their continuous quest for wealth and property has not worked.

I shall now expand on the idea of a different strategy or a road less travelled, with faith in God and prayer, combined with the intersession of Our Lady of Holy Hope.

However, prior to that, I want to make a further comment on technology and global warming, and how technology can be positively used as a tool to save the planet.

CHAPTER 10

CHOICES AND HUMAN NATURE

The choices we make reveal the true Nature of our character

Life is full of choices from the time we rise each day, to when we close our eyes each night.

In the previous chapter, I suggested a number of changes in humanity's lifestyle/behaviour which would, in my opinion, help in our battle against global warming.

I might have sounded anti-technological, but it was not my intention to do so.

I am very aware of the part technology plays in life and especially in Manufacturing Engineering.

Indeed, one of the subjects I teach in Griffith College Limerick is Advanced Manufacturing Technology.

Teaching this subject has enlightened my awareness of the 4th Industrial Revolution, where advances in the areas of artificial intelligence, energy storage, robotics and quantum computing, are real, and will have a huge impact on the world, to the advancement of human experience and quality of life in the years to come.

A recent, major breakthrough in the construction industry has been Contour Crafting. This is a process that has the potential to revolutionise the construction industry. Dr Behrokh Khoshnevis, of the University of Southern California, has invented *a machine that prints houses*[55]. Another term for this is the 3 D printing of a house. Due to an expected reduced construction time from months to days, the CO_2 e emissions involved in the construction will be greatly reduced.

Returning to Genesis, I once again ponder… *God saw everything that he had made, and indeed, it was very good*[56].

Therefore, if creation (humanity) has the potential to be very good and the choices we make reflect this very good character, I am full of hope that humanity will make the correct choices in its efforts to save the planet from global warming.

We simply must be careful how we use this advanced technology, from i-phones to robotics to quantum computing, to *contour crafting*[57].

What should our focus be, living on a planet that is heating up, which contains 4th Industrial Revolution technology?

In my opinion, we should focus on the use of this latest technology to find ways of doing tasks in a shorter time period, speeding up

---

[55] Lefteri, C. p. 242

[56] Gen. 1:31

[57] Lefteri, C. p. 243

manufacturing processes, where less energy is used, which will result in greater production per unit of energy used (energy efficiency).

Reiterating the potential very good character of humanity I have mentioned, we should use energy more wisely and not waste it on meaningless social media playtime.

Technology can be one of humanity's tools to help deal with the ravages of global warming.

If this happens and we make the correct choices regarding energy use that reflects the potential very good nature of the human character, I am hopeful that we are on the right path to save the planet... choosing the correct strategy that will lead towards a sustainable future..

CHAPTER 11

FAITH

Faith starts when your
knowledge ends

We have reams of scientific knowledge highlighting the causes and possible solutions to the problem of global warming (apart from current R & D developments yet to be announced).

We have travelled along a path influenced by politics and economics for many years, and I feel we have in all probability come to its proverbial "end point".

Is there another possible road, a road less travelled that can lead us to a more sustainable future?

I feel there is and I have referred to this other plan as a new strategy, a new approach, and I feel it can only come alive in the presence of God and prayer!

In this present world, sometimes described as *post religion post truth*[58], I feel this chapter is going to be the most difficult to write, as

---

[58] Discussion I heard on RTE Radio 1, Ireland

it is about "faith", faith in God, something that is ever present, and is available when all else fails, yet is almost impossible to describe.

St Paul, when writing to the Ephesians approximately 2,000 years ago, was faced with the same problem... as he attempted to describe faith.

For by grace you have been saved through faith, and this is not your own doing: it is the gift of God – not the result of works, so that no one may boast[59].

Faith for Paul was a gift from God.

Would God create humanity, and not present this gift to all?

I believe that this life as we know it is a gift from God, to go beside His gift of faith (faith in God), given freely to all.

Of course, some people claim not to possess this gift of faith. I believe that they take this position, because they never searched for the gift and never experienced the feelings of love and warmth experienced when finding it and unwrapping it.

What about those people who do not believe in the existence of God?

Well, they might not believe in God, but I believe God believes in them.

To all who profess another faith...

---

[59] Eph. 2:8

I believe some Omnipotent Power whose foundation is based on humbleness, love, truth, honesty and justice, (the God of creation), is present in all faiths.

There simply has to be more to this life than… we are born, we live, we try to make enough money to make ourselves comfortable, we strive to have a career that makes a difference, we possibly have a partner/marry, we may have children, then we die and disappear for ever… going into the ground in a box... and that is the end.

There simply must be more… There must be more, because this world and this existence we experience, is simply too mysterious and beautiful to be just a product of a pool of chemicals behaving randomly, excluding the God responsible for it all, the God of creation present in Genesis.

Everything around us is a mystery.

We live on a planet, a rock suspended in space, held in position by gravitational forces involving other planets, hurdling forward in time, at a speed approaching that of light, in an ever-expanding Cosmos... expanding from an event called the *Big Bang, which occurred about fourteen billion years ago*[60].

In this state of mystery, we do know that our sun will become a red giant some day, as it nears the end of its life. At this stage, sometime in the very distant future, all life will cease to exist on this planet, even "life" as small as *viruses and bacteria*[61].

---

[60] Cox, B and Cohen, A. p. 65

[61] Quinlan, H., E. p. 3-4

Uncomfortable... unsure? You should be, especially in the face of such extraordinary mystery.

A photograph taken of planet earth on February 14th 1990, by the Voyager 1 space probe, 6,000,000,000 km (6 billion km) away, resulted in an image of a tiny *Blue Dot* of less than a pixel. This photo inspired the astronomer and author Carl Sagan to write the following... giving us his personal incredible perspective on this planet.

Look again at that dot... that is us. The earth is a very small stage in a vast cosmic arena. Our planet is a lonely speck in the great enveloping cosmic dark. The earth is the only world known so far to harbour life. It has been said that astronomy is a humbling and character-building experience... there is perhaps no better demonstration of the folly of human conceits than this distant image of our tiny world[62].

For Carl Sagan, (who was not a believer in the God of creation), this photograph humbled him and almost made him speechless. However, he saw faith in God as belief in something without evidence, and being the scientist, he always needed proof and evidence.

I respect Sagan's point of view, however I think differently.

I say... in our humble, almost speechless state, let us gain some consolation and comfort that there is a God responsible for this mystery of existence, where we find ourselves on a lump of rock, hurtling at lightning speed, to a place, space and time, where we have not been before, and will never be again.

---

[62] www.planetary.org/worlds/pale-blue-dot

I believe the only constant in this ever-changing energetic, dynamic, spiritual existence is God, the God who loves us, and cares for us... the God of creation.

Of course, Richard Dawkins, like Sagan, would not agree... He dismantles and dismisses the beautifully written texts of the Bible as being primitive stories, written by primitive people... *The whole world is made of incredibly tiny things, much too small to be visible to the naked eye – and yet none of the myths or so-called holy books that some people, even now, think were given to us by an all-knowing god, mentions them at all.* Dawkins continues... *In fact, unsurprisingly, the stories in holy books don't contain any more information about the world than was known to the primitive peoples who first started telling them*[63].

Richard Dawkins, like Sagan, is entitled to his points of view; however, I feel he is over critical of spiritual writings like the Bible. To refer to it as a collection of primitive writings written by primitive people is, in my opinion, simply wrong, and is a gross insult to the billions of people worldwide who believe in the Word of God and find comfort in it.

Stephen Hawking asked the question *is there a God?*[64], in his book, *Brief Answers To The Big Questions.* He continued by pondering the God of creation... his answer after years of research in the areas of quantum physics cosmology was as follows...

But of course the critical question is raised again: did God create the quantum laws that allowed the Big Bang to occur? In a nutshell,

---

[63] Dawkins, R. p. 95

[64] Hawkins, S. p. 23

do we need a God to set it up so that the Big Bang could bang? I have no desire to offend anyone of faith, but I think science has a more compelling explanation than a divine creator[65].

I shall now park Hawking, Dawkins and Sagan, while thanking God for the spiritual happiness and contentment I have attained, by searching, finding, unwrapping and exploring God's gift of faith freely given to me.

I cannot mention God without mentioning love.

St Augustine, in one of his many writings, confirms this fact.

As Saint John himself expresses it more clearly: "God is love, and he who abides in love abides in God, and God abides in him". It is not enough to say... "Love comes from God". Which of us would dare to say what Saint John said: "God is love"? He knew what he was saying, for he experienced this love himself[66].

This reminds me of the final line from the musical Les Miserables... *To love another person, is to see the face of God*[67].

Before I share my gift of faith in God, I would like to share the thoughts of the singer/songwriter David Bowie (RIP) and his wife Iman, along with a number of astronauts... Bill Anders (and the crew of Apollo 8), and Yuri Gagarin.

---

[65] Ibid, p. 34

[66] The Divine Office of the Church, St Augustine

[67] www.famvin.org/en/2020/09/28/to-love-another-person-is-to-see-the-face-of-god-part-i/

In his 1969 hit, *Space Oddity*, Bowie penned the following lyric... *check ignition and may God's love go with you...*[68] While his wife Iman wrote on the morning of his death... *the struggle is real, but so is God*[69].

The Soviet cosmonaut Yuri Gagarin, the first man to orbit the earth on the 12th of April 1961, proclaimed afterwards in accordance with Marxist materialist dogma... *There is no God to be seen up here*[70].

Yuri, later in his life, became a believer in the God of creation!

Less than a decade after Gagarin orbited the earth, Bill Anders, Frank Borman and Jim Lovell (the crew of Apollo 8), travelled all the way to the moon, where they orbited it a number of times. On the night of December 24th 1968, the following message was broadcast by these men to millions who listened on.

In the beginning, God created the heavens and the Earth. And the Earth was without form, and void; and darkness was upon the face of the deep, while a wind from God swept over the face of the waters. Then God said let there be light, and there was light. And God saw that the light was good and God separated the light from the darkness. God called the light day and the darkness night. And there was evening and there was morning, the first day. And God said, let there be a dome in the midst of the waters, and let it separate the waters from the waters. So God made the dome and separated the waters that were under the dome from the waters that

---

[68] www.genius.com/David-bowie-space-oddity-lyrics

[69] www.mirror.co.uk/3am/celebrity-news/david-bowie-didnt-fear-death-7169844

[70] Kung, H. p. 119

were above the dome. And it was so. God called the dome sky. And there was evening and there was morning the second day. And God said let the waters under the sky be gathered together into one place and let the dry land appear. And it was so. God called the dry land Earth and the waters that were gathered together he called seas. And God saw that it was good[71].

Their message concluded with the following sentiment[72]...

And from the crew of Apollo 8, we close with goodnight, good luck, a Merry Christmas – and God bless all of you, all of you on the (very) good Earth[73].

Aware of my faith in God, I continue...

Faith allows us to interpret the meaning and the mysterious beauty of what is unfolding.

The Spirit of God has filled the universe with possibilities and therefore, from the very heart of things, something new can always emerge[74].

Something new can always emerge...

I feel if we decide to connect with God, something new can emerge... we can increase our chances of solving the problem of global warming, with discipline, as we change our lifestyles... change our behaviour.

---

[71] Gen. 1: 1-10

[72] www.nasa.gov/topics/history/features/apollo_8.html

[73] Cox, B and Cohen, A. p. 24

[74] Pope Francis. p. 45

We shall need God's help (because we will not do it on our own), to gracefully reduce our personal carbon footprint, crushing any delusional thoughts that we may have regarding ownership of the planet and allowing those in the Third World, attempting to exist on one dollar a day, to create for themselves a carbon footprint. With God's help, we must find this balance in life.

At the end of the day, I believe the solution to our present problem will involve grace and faith in God, the creator of everything we see around us and everything unseen.

God saw everything that he had made, and indeed, it was very good[75].

How can we/do we communicate with God?

We can do so through prayer.

What is prayer… is it all words, words and more words?

I say no… words are not needed to pray, as prayer for me personally is simple awareness… awareness as I look at a night sky, gaze at a sunset, or listen to a cuckoo calling out in Miley's meadow Foildearg (a valley near Cappawhite in Co. Tipperary, Ireland) on a calm sunny April day… aware that I am not alone, and this life which I experience, is much more than I perceive or think I understand.

In life, it is sometimes difficult to connect with a busy high-flying person and a better way of connecting is through His mother.

Hence, I now turn to our Lady of Holy Hope, to ask her for help, to find Hope, in this sometimes hopeless global warming crisis.

---

[75] Gen. 1:31

I shall use words this time, as this is a prayer of petition.

O Mary my Mother, I kneel before you with a, truthful heart.

O Mother of mercy, you are all powerful with your divine Son. He can refuse no request of your Immaculate Heart. Show yourself a true Mother to me by being my advocate before His throne. O refuge of sinners and hope of the Hopeless, to whom shall I turn if not to you?

Obtain for me then, O Mother of Hope, the grace of perfect resignation to God's Holy Will and the courage to take up my cross and follow Jesus. Beg of His Sacred Heart the special favour that I ask in this Novena...

(mention your petition here… perhaps one could ask Our Lady for the grace of patience, and the grace to work with others to save the planet, freeing ourselves from the tendency to mislead, in a blind pursuit of wealth and property... the grace to realise that we do not own the planet... the grace to use less energy in our daily lives and of course, the grace to treat the people of the Third World with dignity, respect and fairness).

But above all, I pray O dearest Mother, that through your most powerful intercession, my heart may be filled with Holy Hope, so that in life's darkest hour I may never fail to trust in God my Saviour, but by walking in the way of His commandments, I may merit to be united with Him, and with you in the eternal joys of Heaven, Amen.

Mary, my Hope, have pity on me... Hope of the Hopeless, pray for me[76].

---

[76] Our Lady of Holy Hope Novena prayer, Parish of Cahir, Diocese of Waterford & Lismore Ireland, Thursday May 4th 2017

Grace has been mentioned quite a lot in this chapter... grace is the free and unearned favour of God or a divinely given talent or blessing.

Grace is first and foremost the gift of God, who justifies and sanctifies us[77].

The road less travelled beckons…

---

[77] Catechism of the Catholic Church. p. 435

CHAPTER 12

HUMANS AND VULTURES

Humans wash before eating... vultures after

Today, June 12th, 2020 we live in the era of "wash your hands". The Covid-19 pandemic has been at large since February 2020, and one of the catch phrases has been "wash your hands". We also have social distancing laws and have just come out of a major lockdown.

This meant that most retail stores, factories, non-essential services and businesses were closed... people worked from home or did not work at all. Airlines were grounded worldwide, and major automobile traffic was absent from our motorways.

In Ireland, we could only walk within a 2 km distance from our homes. People over 70 were encouraged to "cocoon", stay in and not mix with others.

This was a life changing experience for all, and a new normal for living in community.

People experienced a silence alien to the world of the 21st century.

People became more aware of the sounds, smells and presence of nature in their lives, especially bird call…

The skies, free of aeroplanes, became cleaner and clearer.

Air quality improved and nature walked freely for the first time in many years, uninterrupted by major harmful anthropogenic greenhouse gas pollutants.

The Irish Government and Governments worldwide willingly made money available for healthcare and hospitals. People who were unable to work got a meaningful "pandemic payment" to keep their personal financial shows on the road. Banks also chipped in, giving temporary relief to customers under pressure to make mortgage repayments.

Humanity showed remarkable levels of goodness, love and kindness, as all worked in harmony to "flatten the curve".

While the Covid-19 pandemic caused pain, hardship and death for many, (may they all rest in peace), it also brought the best out of people.

Many people were content to stay at home and no longer had a need to travel by air or car, because they knew it was the correct thing to do at that moment in time.

A serene type of peace descended on the world.

When people briefly met, the greeting was… "How are you… strange times we are having".

Strange times indeed…

In chapter 9, as part of a proposed new strategy, I made a few suggestions that might help reduce greenhouse gas emissions, which included... reducing air travel by perhaps grounding all airlines one day a week, working from home more and cycling more.

During nature's Covid-19 pandemic, all these lifestyle changes and changes in behaviour I had suggested were taken on, and more...

In chapter 10, I expanded on the topic of technology by mentioning how it could play its part in tackling the global warming crisis, where a decrease or increase in technology could have an impact. Reducing the use of car travel could help, working from home (zoom conferences) could help and web cams could be used to bring Church services to the homes of the world.

During the Covid-19 shutdown, all of the above happened and all had a positive effect on the environment.

Therefore, the encouraging signs are there, that humanity can make necessary changes, if the crisis is big enough.

Why the global warming crisis cannot nudge humanity to make some necessary lifestyle changes is a puzzle to me. Perhaps it can be traced to the human failings of some, sown in Eden many years ago...

So, maybe it is now time for all to stop for a moment and think of the illness, (global warming), affecting the planet!

The effect of this lockdown has led to a decrease in greenhouse gas emissions, due to less travel. However, there is an increase in CO_2 emissions worldwide because of one particular sector... the plastics industry.

Our healthcare workers have had to wear PPE (personal protective equipment) as they worked in hospitals and nursing homes.

This has generated thousands of tonnes of plastic material, only used once, before its disposal for incineration.

When this plastic is destroyed by incineration, the greenhouse gases emitted are dealt with using gas cleaning technology, so when they are destroyed, they do not add to the global warming crisis.

However, the manufacture of this plastic leads to the emission of CO_2.

Of course, the story around this PPE and the countries who successfully obtained it, versus the countries that had problems obtaining it, once again echoed Genesis. This wheeling and dealing involved people of wealth and influence, where their position in life made them perhaps think that they owned something... (the planet?).

The human failing of some sown in Eden, once again raised its head.

It resulted in the First and Second Worlds having adequate supplies of PPE, while the Third World struggled.

There is also the ongoing problem with plastic use in supermarkets. I have noticed loaves of bread and items of fruit, increasingly wrapped in plastic since the emergence of the pandemic.

All this plastic is a worry and a source of greenhouse gas emissions worldwide.

So, even though CO_2 emissions worldwide during Covid-19 have decreased, with reductions of up to 9.5% on Irish carbon emissions, all this extra plastic now being produced, will have a negative effect on the positives gained.

However, humanity's ability to embrace a change in lifestyle/ behaviour during this pandemic is encouraging.

Now, all that is needed, is to convince the world's population that the planet is also suffering from a chronic illness called global warming, and we need to extend and prolong our "new normal" way of living for the planet's sake in the years to come, in our efforts to tackle and overcome this illness.

CHAPTER 13

FRIENDSHIP

For as a man is, so is his friend

At the end of the day, friendship is the most important thing in life... it is so special that it simply cannot be fake or forced. I came across a definition of friendship one time that read... *A friend is someone who asks you how you are, and waits for an answer*[78].

Another sign of true genuine friendship is when a comfortable warm silence can exist between people, where the very act of talking is not necessary.

One of my all-time great genuine friends was John Meagher, who lived just outside Cahir, Co Tipperary.

John (may you rest in peace), was one of the best-read men I ever met... his house had a special room, set up as a library.

I looked at all the books one day and asked him if he had read them all. Smilingly, John replied... "Well I have dipped into them all".

---

[78] www. quotefancy.com/quote/1647944/Grey-Owl-Friends

During John's illness, I took him for a spin one day through the Tipperary/Waterford countryside.

I was driving silently and a car passed, coming from the opposite direction. I saluted the driver and he/she saluted me back. This happened a number of times, with a few different drivers… then John spoke up.

"You know" he said… "the reason we salute in the green country roads goes back to Eden… we are softer in greenery, more human, open and friendlier."

He continued… "you never get this in the concrete jungle of a town or city. The concrete makes us tough, less friendly, less human, closed and less likely to salute the oncomer."

That was John at his best, as we started another wonderful conversation (by the way, he was also a great admirer of St Paul).

John and I went to a Bruce Springsteen concert in Croke Park Dublin, on May 29th 2016. It was John's first time seeing the Boss. He was poorly that evening, and I asked him once too often if he was okay. John, with a big grin on his face replied… "I am not as sick as you think I am Tom".

With a smile, I replied… "Good".

Even though I never personally met Bruce, I have a bond with him, because of my connection with the E-Street band, and my admiration of his talent, music and lyrics down through the years.

Ever since experiencing Slane Castle in 1985, I have been a huge fan.

His autobiography *Born to Run* is a most extraordinary read. Bruce compares life and love, to a tree… *the tree sprouts, its branches thicken, mature, bloom. It is scarred by lightning, shaken by thunder, sickness, human events and God's hand. Drawn black, it grows itself back towards light, rising higher towards heaven while thrusting itself deeper, more firmly, into the earth. Its history and memory retained; its presence felt*[79].

Growing up, Bruce had a favourite copper beech tree in his neighbourhood. He drove back one night and saw that the tree was gone, *but still there*, as he looked up at where it used to stand and remembered it.

Bruce finishes his book with a prayer… *Our Father, who art in heaven, hallowed be thy name. Thy kingdom come, thy will be done, on earth as it is in heaven. Give us this day, our daily bread, and forgive us our trespasses as we forgive those who trespass against us, and lead us not into temptation, but deliver us from evil… all of us, forever and ever amen*[80].

I picked up the Sunday Independent on June 21st, 2020, and saw where Roy Keane (a legend of Irish soccer) was interviewed by Barry Egan. Barry asked Roy if he believed in God… *Yeah, I believe there is something up there looking after me. Absolutely*, replied Roy.

Do you pray? Asked Barry. *Yeah, I have faith. I was brought up with that,* replied Roy[81].

---

[79] Springsteen, B. p. 504

[80] Ibid, p. 505

[81] Egan, B. Sport. p. 3

Barry Egan interviewed Andrea Corr on the Sunday Independent of September 6th 2020. In the article, she shared her thoughts and feelings on faith in God and prayer... *faith is not against reason, it is beyond it...* while she described the church where she prayed as... *the room of love and hope*[82].

Andrea Corr has a connection with God, with prayer and has faith... the same can be said of Roy Keane. My great friend John Meagher had faith in God, and believed in prayer. Bruce Springsteen has faith in God, believes in prayer and remembers a tree in his local neighbourhood.

This book was inspired by faith in God, inspired by prayer and inspired by a mythological/theological tree... the tree of the knowledge of good and evil of Eden, and of course the whole idea of Eden had its genesis in John Meagher's comments on greenery as I drove along the meandering Tipperary/Waterford country roads in early 2016.

Later in the concert, Bruce sang *Born to Run*[83], in a stadium I had the privilege of seeing some of the greatest GAA athletes ever, scoring life changing goals[84].

As Lar Corbett ran back to his position after scoring his third goal in the 2010 All Ireland hurling final, he glanced at the jubilant Tipperary crowd and later penned this sentiment.

---

[82] Egan, B. Living. p. 1

[83] www.irishtimes.com/culture/music/bruce-springsteen-to-play-croke-park-concert-in-may-1.2522291

[84] www.irishexaminer.com/sport/gaa/arid-40043561.html

We Think We Own It!

I wonder if they knew each other and I tried to picture them the next day at work. One lad may be a CEO of a big company, the other running a newsagent's and the tall fella on the right drawing the dole maybe. The young fella beside them may be starting school the next morning, possibly hoping someday he'll get to play in an All Ireland final... And then it hit me. No matter if you're a managing director, keeping a small shop or filling out forms in the labour exchange, these lads are bound together, for seventy minutes and nine or ten times a year, by the same thing – Tipperary hurling[85].

Yes... a life changing moment for the goal scorer... but also an opportunity for supporters young and old, (no matter what their situations in life are), to experience a moment of harmony[86].

Thinking of all those life changing moments, as the stadium rocked and rolled, I thought to myself... humanity can also run, rock and roll towards a sustainable planet.

With the help of God, through genuine friendship, prayer and self-discipline, we too can experience a life changing moment... by changing our collective lifestyles, by living in harmony with each other and with nature, and by using less energy.

A life changing moment that will save the planet, as we cleanse ourselves of the dark traits of humanity sown in Eden. Those dark traits that lead to our delusionary thought that we think we own the planet, and results in our ability to mislead others in our quest for wealth and property.

---

[85] Lawlor, D. p. 278

[86] Gen. 2: 25

It is entirely up to us.

Our Lady of Holy Hope pray for all humanity, (both believers in God and non-believers).

CHAPTER 14

WEALTH

Wealth is not in having great possessions, but in having few wants

This has been quite a journey... As I continue; I realise I now have two plans on the table... two strategies. In the last chapter, I thought I had completed my journey by promoting a new strategy based on God and prayer.

However, I find myself back typing today.

I am reminded of a scene from Fiddler of the Roof, which I was part of, in the Marian Hall, Tipperary Town, over twenty years ago.

I was the character of Avrahm, as I stood in conversation with Tevye and two other characters.

One character spoke up and Tevye said... "You are right". A second character spoke, having a different point of view; however Tevye turned to him and said... "You are right". Then I spoke up and asked Tevye... "How can they both be right?" ... To which Tevye replied... "You too are right".

In that scene, we were all right, although we had differing points of view.

As I continue my journey, I am now of the opinion that both strategies are valid and a combination of the best parts of both can go a long way towards solving the global warming crisis.

The strategies I speak of are based on politics, science and economics... and inspired by prayer and the grace of God, along with the intersession of Our Lady of Holy Hope.

I believe we need to change our lifestyles/behaviours; we need to reduce our personal carbon footprint and we need to take a different road in life, where we become more aware of the energy we use daily... we need to get into the habit of not always taking the high energy option... and of course we need to realise that we exist on this planet for the time span of our lives, without ever owning it.

In the reality that not all humanity are Catholic and not all believe in God, I now feel when speaking of my "prayer and grace of God strategy" that it simply is not enough. I feel I must cast my net further in all directions to include all of humanity... Catholic, Christian, members of the Jewish faith (remember Jesus, His mother Mary and His original followers were Jews), other world religions/beliefs and those with no belief in God.

Therefore, we can all change our personal lifestyles/behaviours with the help of prayer, grace and belief in God, or by tapping into our innate natural human goodness mentioned in some philosophical writings. Of course, we can also make these changes by engaging with other world religions/beliefs...

Jim Stynes (RIP), *one of the great Irish sportsmen* (Brian O'Driscoll), embraced all world religions/belief systems during his illness... *I believe there is something to be gained from learning about the religions of the world. I could not understand why people would close their minds to something like the Bhagavad Gita, for example, the Hindu scripture that some scholars believe to be twice as old as the Bible... Various religions and spiritual practices explore ways to become a better person if you are open to accepting their wisdom*[87].

Turning to philosophy, Jean-Jacques Rousseau wrote about humanity's innate natural goodness, in the 18th century... *human beings were born good... man/woman is naturally good, loving justice and order*[88].

I believe the best parts of both strategies combined with the philosophical thought of Rousseau can be used as we journey towards sustainability. Politicians, scientists, engineers, economists and other professionals working as a multidisciplinary team, along with humanity's belief in God, grace, prayers, innate goodness, belief in other world religions and self-awareness can save the planet.

As I have already stated faith in God is a gift, but faith in humanity's innate goodness to do good, to be mindful, honest and truthful, is also a gift.

If prayer helps you... pray. If you would rather search for the innate goodness in humanity, as part of humanity... do that... or if you would rather take the political/academic route, do that...

---

[87] Green, W. p. 309

[88] Magee, B. p. 127-129

The world needs our help, and this is truer today than at any other time in our history… we need to… awaken and connect personally, interpersonally, and as a global society with the innate goodness of ourselves, humanity, society, and the environment in which we live to address the challenges of global warming[89].

Perhaps some of humanity could combine faith in God and prayer, (including faith in other world religions//beliefs), with innate goodness and mindfulness, combined with politics and academia to change their behaviour…

The outcome should be the same, where (we), the First, Second and Third Worlds would gather together metaphorically in harmony, in the mythological/theological Eden, where we would look out for each other, where the ability of some to mislead others in their quest for wealth and property would be no more, and where we would all live with a reduced carbon footprint, in a place we dare not think we own.

This will mean living in a new normal, with eyes on a new type of wealth, a wealth defined by having few wants, and more love… love for the beautiful home freely given to us, a planet that isn't owned by anyone, a planet that just simply lives, and is found on the meandering pathway of the road less travelled.

---

[89] Maull, A., F.

CHAPTER 15

TRUTH

The Truth will make you free.
(Jesus Christ)

I shall begin this chapter by turning to another singer/songwriter...
Gavin James. In a radio interview I once heard involving Gavin, the
topic of truth came up. The interviewer asked him what inspired
him to write lyrics. His answer was most profound in its honesty
and simplicity... *Every song has to have meaning, or else I would
not be telling the truth*[90].

As I began Chapter 11, I described the world as a "post religion post
truth" place... a reality that can lead to an uncomfortable feeling.
Belief in God is waning and it is getting increasingly more difficult
to find truth in the many discussions going on worldwide, in political
and economic circles, on the topic of global warming.

However, despite the waning belief in God, I believe humanity is
still potentially very good and can uphold truth, if we succeed in
connecting with the core of what it means to be human... the innate
goodness we are all born with (Rousseau).

---

[90] shop.gavinjamesmusic.com

I shall now summarise the important truths/untruths highlighted in this small book.

It is true that most harmful greenhouse gases have been produced by humanity burning fossil fuels.

One of the greatest truths of all is that coal should remain in the ground.

Remaining with energy production... low carbon, renewable energy sources must be promoted, while R&D (research and development) in this area should always be well funded by World Governments... this is a definite truth.

I personally believe that it is not a truth to speak ill of and blame the dumb animals for producing methane and carbon dioxide, as they digest grass. What they produce... meat and dairy products, are a miracle of creation and are necessary for feeding humanity.

It is not a true claim, that simply building houses near public transport will help in the battle against global warming... the building materials used and the design is also vitally important to counteract global warming... this is a fact which mainly goes unsaid.

It is true that wind must be promoted as a renewable energy source, but the truth that wind turbines on hill tops are not aesthetically gratifying, remains unsaid.

The truth about CCS (carbon capture and storage) and how it can help the global warming crisis mainly goes unsaid.

The truth that we need to lower our personal carbon footprint and reduce our personal energy consumption is not being said enough by our politicians and world leaders, (apart from Pope Francis). *At the same time, on the national and local levels, much still needs to be done, such as promoting ways of conserving energy*[91].

Advertisements promoting brand new hybrid cars and electric cars as an aid in the battle against global warming are not totally truthful. The indirect CO_2 e produced during the manufacture and assembly of these new cars is not openly acknowledged. In my opinion, it is better to drive your old petrol car for a few more years, instead of scrapping it and blindly purchasing a brand new electric or hybrid, (petrol/electric) car.

The mythological serpent of Eden (Satan, the dark prince of lies), spoke the greatest untruth of all... *You will not die; your eyes will be opened*[92].

The unfortunate truth that the oceans are becoming more acidic is accurate.

The unfortunate truth that political talk and agreements from Kyoto to Paris have not resulted in a reduction in CO_2 e emissions in any way is accurate.

The unfortunate truth that the people of the Third World are largely ignored when it comes to global warming discussions is accurate.

The truth that we must take a *road less travelled*[93] and change our lifestyles/personal behaviours goes unsaid.

---

[91] Pope Francis. p. 93

[92] Gen. 3:4-5

[93] Peck, M.,S.

The truth that the production of the plastics involved in wrapping food items and in the manufacturing of PPE (personal protective equipment), due to the Covid-19 pandemic, is a huge emitter of carbon dioxide goes unsaid.

Finally, the greatest truth of all has not been mentioned in this global warming debate, (except for Pope Francis)... we do not own the planet... we simply pass through this existence without ever owning it. *The created things of this world are not free of ownership... 'for they are yours, O Lord, who love the living, (Wis. 11:26)*[94].

At the trial of Jesus approximately 2,000 years ago, truth was impossible to attain. His Words as He stood before Pilate, highlighted this fact... *I came into the world to testify for the truth... everyone who belongs to the truth listens to my voice*[95].

If truth flowed freely in Jesus' heart, what I wonder was going on in the hearts of all who stood by watching?

Pilate, one of the most powerful men (by human standards), in the gathering showed how troubled he was within his heart, as he asked... *What is truth?*[96]

I believe that a type of blockage occurred, in the hearts of all present at this trial. This resulted in a type of paralysis, which prevented them from shouting "STOP"... preventing them from backing Jesus. For some reason, they did not really want to get involved, they remained passive, calm almost... silent... they were in a way, emotionally disconnected from what was happening before their eyes.

---

[94] Pope Francis. p. 49

[95] Jn. 18: 37

[96] Jn. 18: 38

Using a little Latin… *Et cognoscetis veritatem et veritas liberabit vos… and you will know the truth, and the truth will make you free*[97]…

Truth, if practiced by humanity, can make us act with freedom, enabling us to look up from our self-centred wealth driven lives, to take notice of our suffering planet and take unselfish steps to pave a pathway towards its redemption.

Mark Barret speaks of freedom… *Letting go of my own will has to be the most dynamic way of entering into freedom*[98].

Freedom can therefore be obtained from letting go of one's own will and letting go of the desire for wealth and property, whose seed was sown in Eden by our first mythological parents. In other words, we must become aware of the reality that we do not own the planet.

Of course… we are all entitled to a roof over our heads, but when one allows oneself to become a slave to wealth and property and to mislead others in its quest, it becomes a problem… (recalling Satan, who was the first to mislead).

Professor Michael Mullins, a priest of the diocese of Waterford & Lismore Ireland, when speaking of *freedom through the truth*, refers to how Jewish Rabbis *spoke of the Law as a liberating experience, freeing one from worldly care*[99].

---

[97] Jn. 8:32

[98] Barrett, M. p. 112

[99] Mullins, M. p. 230

Returning to Jesus... in my mind's eye I can imagine Him saying, as he leads us towards a sustainable planet... *Awake sleeper, I have not made you to be held a prisoner* of darkness and untruths[100].

On the first Holy Saturday, as Jesus lay in the tomb, Our Lady spent the day in the upper room consoling and praying with the disillusioned Apostles. She never gave up hope that something good would happen (Our Lady of Holy Hope mentioned in chapter 11).

Of course, for believers, something never seen before or since happened, the Resurrection... an event that changed the world for ever.

I now once again, turn to the very important group of humanity, who live on this planet and do not believe in Jesus Christ, Christian prayer or the Resurrection. This does not concern me in the least, as I accept and respect their current position on their journey through life.

However, I do hope that they believe in one vital thing... I hope they believe in the innate goodness of humanity that Rousseau mentioned in his writings of over 250 years ago, and in the innate good character that is the human character... a goodness that if tapped into, can ultimately lead to truth, honesty and freedom.

Continuing with Rousseau and his philosophical writing, let us go a little deeper... *human beings were born good but were corrupted by the experience of growing up in society... a child growing up in a so-called civilised society is taught to curb and frustrate his/her natural instincts*[101].

---

[100] The Divine Office Vol II p. 320

[101] Magee, B. p. 127

Rousseau believed that humanity's natural instinct or state of nature was one of innocence, like the naive innocent Eve, before the serpent misled her. *The state of nature is the hypothetical, prehistoric place and time where human beings live uncorrupted by society*[102].

Rousseau highlights a very important fact of life, a fact that is a reality for the believer and non-believer in God. We are all born good until the influences of the world can make some of us careful, cautious, closed, and in some cases hard… displaying a hardness of heart, where we frustrate our innocent, good natural instincts.

His theory/hypothesis resonates with… my thoughts/hypothesis… the paralysis of heart (of some of humanity) which originated in Eden.

Rousseau *contended that the establishment of property and government had deformed our nature*… echoes of the dark trait of humanity, sown in Eden… thinking that we own the planet[103].

Of course, Rousseau, in other works alternately emphasised the shortfalls of his state of nature. However, this book is not meant to be a critique of Rousseau's philosophical thought… I simply want to highlight one aspect of Rousseau's state of nature that resonates with our first parent's existence in Eden[104], which was one of harmony[105] with nature and themselves, before the disrupting evil serpent entered their lives.

---

[102] www.sparknotes.com/philosophy/rousseau/themes/

[103] Mautner, T. p. 491

[104] Mythology/Theology

[105] Gen. 2: 25

Psalm 133 of the Old Testament shows the joy associated with siblings or friends living together in unity and harmony.

How very good and pleasant it is when the kindred live together in unity... it is like the dew of Hermon which falls on the mountains of Zion[106].

This psalm, written many years ago, highlights the joy which radiates from human hearts, when people, full of truth, honesty and freedom, live in unity, love and harmony together. Of course, this "utopia" can be difficult to attain in life, and when it is attained, it must be continuously worked on to be maintained.

After the Resurrection, and inspired by the Holy Spirit, the followers of Jesus lived in such unity and harmony.

For humanity (both believers in God, and nonbelievers), truth can flow freely through their collective hearts if they genuinely wish to allow it... where, in the words of Gavin James, we would act with "meaning", where all would finally see the reality of the crisis that is global warming and decide to do something positive to counteract it.

---

[106] The Harper Collins Study Bible, psalm 133. p. 924

CHAPTER 16

THE SOUTHERN CROSS

When it is dark, look for the stars

Our cumulative thinking needs to change... our mindset and our hearts need to change.

We need to break this tendency towards paralysis that can surface within our human hearts from time to time, or as Rousseau would say... our corruption due to the influence of the world and society.

This brings me to what I consider the heart of the matter, or crux, which drives global warming... a type of paralysis within the hearts of some of humanity, which was sown in Eden, when the serpent misled Eve and when Adam thought he owned the fruit, the tree and the Garden. This crux was also present within the hearts of the onlookers at the trial of Jesus... and is presently within the hearts of some State and Church leaders today, when they fail to stand up for truth.

The term crux is derived from the Latin for cross (the tree that Jesus was crucified on). This connects the present inaction of some of humanity regarding the crisis that is global warming, back to the tree of Eden and the Cross of Calvary.

We live in a society, where sometimes the so-called best, wisest action to take, is to remain silent... even when witnessing great injustices... to be cool, closed and emotionally disconnected, is the admired action to take.

Silence of course, can be full of light or totally dark.

A silence containing the light of truth, is the silence the injured party partakes in (the person who suffered the injustice), after he/she pleads his/her innocence and waits respectfully for a genuine apology.

A silence containing the total darkness of untruth on the other hand, is the silence that the person who caused the hurt may partake in. This un-Godly silence could easily be overcome by a genuine honest apology, and the proclamation of "sorry" in an atmosphere of genuine empathy and remorse, recognising the hurt and injustice caused. However, a blockage within that person's human heart, the crux that fans global warming can stop this from happening.

Indeed, after Adam and Eve had disobeyed God, after the serpent (Satan) misled them, causing them to have the delusional thoughts of thinking that they had ownership of Eden and its fruit, I feel they could still have genuinely apologised... instead they hid from God.

They heard the sound of the Lord God walking in the garden at the time of the evening breeze, and the man and his wife hid themselves from the presence of the Lord God among the trees of the garden[107].

This image of "hiding" is still very much present in our world today, as some of humanity persistently hide behind their lies and untruths, in a dark silence.

Before hiding, they reached out and grabbed fig leaves from a tree, an action continued by some of humanity today as they continually grab the resources of the planet for monetary gain, as if they owned it.

Then the eyes of both were opened, they knew they were naked; and they sewed fig leaves together and made loin-cloths for themselves[108].

Years after the events of Eden, when Jesus was condemned to death, one of the first men (St Peter wept in the courtyard)[109], who showed genuine sorrow and remorse, and showed that his emotions were far from repressed, was the much maligned and far from perfect Judas, when he genuinely confessed the wrong he had done.

When Judas, His betrayer, saw that Jesus was condemned, he repented and brought back the thirty pieces of silver to the chief priests and elders. He said "I have sinned by betraying innocent blood"[110].

---

[107] Gen. 3:8

[108] Gen. 3:7

[109] Mt. 26:75

[110] Mt. 27:3-4

So, I definitely would not condemn Judas for the horrible evil act he carried out when betraying Jesus, because, in my opinion, his honest, open, truthful confession cleansed his Soul of any loss of light at that moment in time.

Of course, as Judas approached the Chief Priests with the thirty pieces of silver in his fist, he did so leaving the angry noisy mob in his wake. He acted with freedom away from the mob, whereas the mob remained imprisoned as they "thrived" and wallowed in the power of mob mentality.[111]

A mob, by its nature is made up of some people who just join in the excitement and fun (for them)... just for the *craic*[112]. Some of this mob were probably young people... being egged on by the adults present. The shocking reality is that a section of this mob probably never met Jesus, knew nothing about Him and certainly did not understand the consequences of their actions.

Mobs can vary in size from two people to hundreds or thousands of people. No matter its size, a mob is energised and activated by the same driving forces, a total lack of feeling, an utter lack of respect for and a shocking lack of empathy towards the victim.

After the chaos involving the mob dissipates, the great paradox is that these individuals can return to their normal lives, return to their families and children... showing love and empathy towards them, oblivious to the turmoil they caused when they were part of the mob.

---

[111] O'Shea, J. p. 103

[112] Irish term for carefree fun

This, in my opinion, is a confirmation of the emotional disconnection they had to the events they partook in while under the influence of the mob... events which resulted in the victim being nailed to the proverbial cross.

It is as if they rationalised their behaviour while being part of the mob, as being justified and normal at that moment in time... such is the astonishing power of mob mentality.

In the true knowledge that the remorseful Judas returned to the Chief Priests and threw the thirty pieces of silver on the floor of the temple confessing the wrong he had done[113]... yet another paradox arises for me, as I journey towards the conclusion of this book. Assuming that no one is perfect, and *all have done wrong from time to time*[114], I now share my paradoxical thought, in the form of a question...

Should some of our leaders in Church and State, perhaps consider becoming a little bit more like (the far from perfect but truthful) Judas... a man who had many problems in life, but ultimately came good in the end, as he found his own personal moment of truth before he breathed his last breath on this planet?

Having pondered all this, it is my personal opinion that Judas is now at peace in Heaven!

A letter, text or email, written/sent to any person in authority, in Church or State, deserves recognition and respect. If it is never responded to, or if the response is nothing more than "*I am at a*

---

[113]https://www.rembrandtpaintings.com/judas-returning-the-thirty-pieces-of-silver.jsp

[114] St Paul's letter to the Romans 3:23

loss[115]", without clarification or explanation, then it is obvious that, that person in authority is clearly avoiding the truth concerning the issues at hand. If any of these two scenarios happen, it is a clear sign (in my opinion), that the heart of that person in authority is not as open and honest as the heart of Judas at the end of his life's journey.

I say State and Church... I can write this with 100% conviction, because of shocking extremely dark incidences and stories I have discovered in my research and reading for this book... happenings accompanied by a deafening graceless silence, an un-Godly shrewd silence where the Holy Spirit is absent... a silence signifying the absence of honesty, openness, truth, freedom and the light of God... and this silence can sometimes last a lifetime and beyond.

It was in the midst of a similar silence, that the historical Jesus said nothing, but simply acted approximately 2,000 years ago, as He humbly walked away from the mob towards Calvary, with the cross crushing His shoulder...

I am well aware that one might ask... what silence... sure with the chaotic angry mob shouting, how could there have been silence as Jesus faced towards Calvary?

The silence I refer to, is the worst type... it is the silence very much present, in spite of the noisy, angry chaos in the air... a stony silence that cuts through noise, chaos and shouting, because it symbolises utter lies, dishonesty and untruths.

I once again refer to the world renowned musical, *Les Miserables* where the image of Jesus facing towards Calvary is brilliantly echoed in the magnificent chorus *One Day More*.

---

[115] www.collinsdictionary.com/dictionary/english/at-a-loss

One day more... another day, another destiny, on this never-ending road to Calvary[116].

Our bodies play a central role in our spiritual lives. From the earliest days of the Church, the word Spirit referred quite literally to the Breath of God... "Spiritus" is Latin for breath. Physically, we live because of our breath, which moves in and out of us... we cannot own our breath... the air in our lungs is only there temporarily. Early Christians recognised that our bodily breath was related to the Breath of God ... and not owning the breath we require to remain living, is a constant reminder to us that we do not own this planet!

As the historical Jesus stood at His trial, He said very little... He did not waste His breath. He knew that the Holy Spirit was not present in the hearts of the onlookers. He knew He would be wasting His time, wasting His breath... wasting the breath of God if he had tried to defend Himself.

Saint Catherine of Siena, if she still walked this planet would be outraged... *speak the truth in a million voices, it is silence that kills*[117].

If you ever go to the Southern hemisphere and look to the heavens on a clear night, you will see an image of a crux. The constellation Crux "the Cross", also referred to as the Southern Cross, is clearly visible in the night sky on a clear night.

So, one could say that the paralysis of some, which fans global warming, is written in the stars.

---

[116] www.azlyrics.com/lyrics/lesmiserablescast/onedaymore.html

[117] Wheatley, M. J.

In my opinion, World leaders and Government leaders, should be advising us to curtail certain aspects of our lives, aspects that use a lot of energy... they should be encouraging us to use precious energy more sparingly.

However, I feel they are not facing up to their responsibilities... they are not facing up to the truth of the situation.

I feel a change of heart or *metanoia*[118] is needed. This change of heart may be actualised if we allow ourselves to tap into the good human nature that we were all born with (Rousseau), not allowing our natural instincts to be frustrated by society, which has the potential to mould us differently.

We can also (if we desire) turn to the Holy Spirit, through the intersession of Our Lady of Holy Hope to bring about this change... or, we can do so by engaging in other world religions/beliefs that we may be a part of. Whatever means we choose; I feel it is possible for humanity to bring about this change.

All strategic policy I (we) have engaged in so far, during this journey, has now converged at one point... that is at the crossroads of truth, honesty and light.

Let us accept the mysterious ever changing, river of change that is creation, and that Heraclitus wrote about over 2,600 years ago. Let us not attempt to control what is unpredictable and unpossessable... let us free ourselves from those delusional thoughts and feelings sown in Eden... (thinking that we own the planet).

---

[118] Mautner, T. p. 350

I stood in St Michael's cemetery in Tipperary Town today... it was a warm July day in 2020. Listening to the priest saying the prayers as all present stood socially distancing, I experienced a special, private, personal moment, where I contemplated life, nature, death, global warming and of course resurrection from the dead.

The priest spoke the words I have pondered many times... *we are but dust, and into dust we shall return*[119]. As he did so, I looked up and noticed wind turbines gently turning on a nearby hill... renewable energy, I noticed the greenery of the fields and trees nearby... echoes of Eden and I looked around the gathering and became aware of the possible belief and unbelief in God. The whole mix was there, including the innate goodness of basic human nature (Rousseau).

As the coffin was lowered into the ground... I became aware of how close we all are to the planet. When we die, we will all become one, existing in harmony[120] with the dust and clay of the earth.

Personally, I find the sight of a mound of fresh clay on a newly covered grave to be a powerful image, full of hope and theological optimistic *expectation*[121]. I see it as an image of an expectant ground, with the hopeful, optimistic expectation of rebirth or resurrection for all the Souls of the *very good*[122] people lying within... where they will exist happily ever after, together in heaven, in a state of eternal peaceful harmony for all eternity.

---

[119] Gen. 3:19

[120] Gen. 2:25

[121] Rom. 8:19

[122] Gen. 1:31

The inevitability that we will all become one with the dust and clay of this planet was brought home to me one summer's day, back in 2010 as I stood in Tome cemetery in Co. Tipperary. On entering the cemetery gateway, if you turn left and walk a short distance (approximately thirty steps), you will see an inscription written on a headstone which is dated 1860.

Remember man, as you pass by,
As you are now, so once was I,
As I am now, so you will be,
Remember man Eternity[123].

If the story of the solving of the global warming crisis occurred in a perfect world... humanity would journey with freedom on its pilgrim way, across the landscape of life, along the road less travelled, to the summit where the flag of trust and mutual respect would be planted. In this state of mutual respect, we would live in truth, love and harmony, happily ever after, on a sustainable planet.

If this perfect world scenario was reality, humanity would, without hesitation, come together to create the platform to save the planet... they would, to borrow a phrase from monastic times... be prepared to *sing from the same hymn sheet*[124].

However, in this presently imperfect world, we have a bit to go before this can ever happen.

---

[123] Words written on a headstone, Tome cemetery, Co. Tipperary

[124] www.collinsdictionary.com/dictionary/english/to-be-singing-from-the-same-hymn-sheet

In late July 2020, there was a special European Council held in Brussels. Truth was mentioned in the lead up... *EU's moment of truth as leaders seek COVID funding deal*[125].

The logo advertising this council was... Repair Reform Remodel.

The agenda included discussions on money allocation to help Europe recover from the outbreak of Covid-19... loans and grants for businesses, and details as to how loans would have to be repaid. The outcome of these talks was very good, as repayments would start in 2026... allowing all economies in Europe an opportunity to breathe.

Another positive outcome of these discussions was that it was expected that 30% of funding would target climate-related projects... the EU's objective of climate neutrality by 2050... the EU's climate targets and the Paris Agreement were still being spoken about and are still alive in the hearts and minds of EU leaders.

This is good news.

It gives me hope that European leaders (inspired by the Holy Spirit and Christian prayer, philosophy or other world religions/beliefs), can act in the correct way. Hope that perhaps the human failings of some, sown in Eden, are beginning to show signs of healing... allowing humanity to make the correct decisions in response to the reality and dangers of global warming... reflecting the truth that is hopefully beginning to flow freely through human hearts.

---

[125] www.bbc.com/news/world-europe-53429064

If this happens at a family/community level, it is my hope that it will spread to a national level, national politics and international politics.

If influential politicians act with truth flowing freely through their collective hearts, the leaders of the USA, Russia, China and other countries, might eventually begin to treat each other with mutual respect and dignity, and decide to interact in a harmonic way with each other. I know this sounds far-fetched, but we simply cannot lose hope.

In early August 2020, I came across a very disturbing article on the web... Tensions between China and the United States had reached the most acute levels of disfunctionality since the countries normalised diplomatic relations more than four decades ago.

Craig Allen, president of the US-China Business Council, said that he was alarmed by the increasing invective actions from two Superpowers that together represent 40% of global economic output... *if we are yelling at each other and slamming doors, then the world is a very unstable place, and businesses are not able to plan*[126].

This is extremely worrying. The image of mature, well-educated members of this joint US-China Business Council yelling at each other and slamming doors is not good.

In my opinion, the world would be a healthier, more open, truthful and honest place if world leaders were yelling at each other and

---

[126] www.nytimes.com/2020/07/22/world/asia/us-china-cold-war.html

slamming doors in their frustration over the current global warming crisis.

Instead, a cool careful silence exists regarding this crisis, where politicians remain emotionally disconnected and do not say much. They seem as emotionally disconnected as the mob who looked on as Jesus was condemned to death.

No one in political circles is getting as animated or vocal about this crisis as Greta Thunberg and her young supporters. Named as Time's person of the year[127], Greta has a good heart... she is not afraid to speak out and is not emotionally disconnected in a cautious silence... she is not afraid to show *passion*[128].

Greta's truth and honesty makes her free to speak her mind, when it comes to the "pandemic" that is global warming.

I am well aware that Greta, and her generation, might not totally agree with what I propose regarding the use of i-phones and smart-phones.

However, I do believe that they are in tune with the remainder of what I propose, i.e. a change of heart (metanoia) in humanity, a change in lifestyle (behaviour), which can lead to a reduction in our personal carbon footprint and of course an acknowledgement of the reality that we do not own the planet.

Humanity needs more people like Greta to awaken us from our imprisonment, due to the crux or paralysis within the hearts of some.

---

[127] www.time.com/person-of-the-year-2019-greta-thunberg/

[128] Descartes, R.

We can't save the world by playing by the rules, because the rules have to change. Everything needs to change – and it has to start today (Greta Thunberg)[129].

Echoes of the need for a change of heart or metanoia that I have mentioned...

Despite this rather negative ending, I do hope that this little book clearly spells out the precarious position we all find ourselves in, precarious but hopeful that things will improve, because the human heart is forever hopeful, and I write this with genuine *meaning* (Gavin James)...

I am personally hopeful, that we will eventually come to the realisation that "we do not inherit the earth from our ancestors, we bequeath to our children" (chapter 2); in other words, we do not own the planet.

My hope continues that we will realise that a reduction in energy used/consumed, will result in a reduced personal carbon footprint (chapter 4), which will go a long way towards solving the crisis that is global warming.

Of course, this is easier said than done... it will involve a change in lifestyle and a change of heart (metanoia), where we will decide to travel less and fundamentally reduce our personal standard of living. Holidaying at home more, not being obsessed with purchasing a new car every year and reducing smart-phone and i-phone usage, are some of the changes we are fundamentally expected to contemplate and carry out.

---

[129] www.curious.earth/blog/greta-thunberg-quotes-best-21/

I am also hopeful that Greta Thunberg and other global warming activists, will not be wasting their collective breaths as they speak out in defence of this beautiful silent planet... a planet whose silence is grace-filled, God filled, radiant with light, where the Holy Spirit resides, where the dark evil serpent of Eden (Satan) is unwelcome... a silence where honesty, openness, truth and mutual freedom resides in a spirit of genuine friendship, love, respect, freedom and harmony... a silence that reflects the mind and heart of the historical Jesus as He put His shoulder under the cross and faced towards Calvary, leaving the angry, out of control mob in His wake!

Let us look to the mysterious stars for inspiration, as we, with hope create a platform to crush the dark crux driving global warming and by doing so, allow the planet to once again return to a state of sustainability... reflecting the original *very good*[130] creation that was Eden before the evil serpent appeared on the scene. A state of sustainability... where in the words of St Paul, the breath of Jesus will finally overcome all darkness[131].

This reminds me of the very old song, *Beautiful Isle of Somewhere*[132], written by Jessie Brown Pounds and Sylvester Fearis in 1897. This was a song inspired by the Book of Revelation, and the image of the new Jerusalem (which can be interpreted as a sustainable planet), coming down from the heavens, where... *the city has no need of sun or moon to shine on it, for the glory of God is its light, and its lamp is the Lamb*[133].

---

[130] Gen. 1:31

[131] 2 Thessalonians 2:8

[132] library.timelesstruths.org/music/Beautiful_Isle_of_Somewhere/

[133] Rev. 21:23

It contains imagery of all *being well*, a land of *truth*, a place where the *human heart is stronger*, and a place where *angels wait*...

Somewhere the sun is shining,
Somewhere the songbirds dwell.
Hush then thy sad repining,
God lives and all is well.

Refrain.
Somewhere, somewhere,
Beautiful Isle of somewhere.
Land of the true, where we live anew,
Beautiful Isle of somewhere.

Somewhere the day is longer,
Somewhere the task is done.
Somewhere the heart is stronger,
Somewhere the guerdon won.

Somewhere the load is lifted,
Close by an open gate.
Somewhere the clouds are rifted,
Somewhere the angels wait.

CHAPTER 17

LIFE

Life can only be understood backwards, but it must be lived forwards
(Soren Kierkegaard)

Today is January 20th 2021, President Joe Biden's inauguration day. Before I talk about the new President, I want to briefly comment on President Trump. As I think about Trump, I am reminded of a radio interview given by the Irish poet Brendan Kennelly (RIP)[134] a number of years ago. He met a man one day in a pub, and the man asked him what he did during his life. Brendan replied and said... "I did a little teaching". Brendan then returned the question. The man paused and thought for a moment, then he said... "I did my best".

In the spirit of dignity, respect and fairness, I sum up President Trump's time in the Whitehouse as a four year period where he simply "did his best".

Now to President Biden's inauguration ceremony... As it happened during a Covid-19 level 5 shutdown in Ireland and as I was working

---

[134] Kennelly, B.

from home, I had ample time to light a fire, sit down and watch this unique moment unfolding... (I burned wood in the stove, with a little turf).

As the occasion took shape and as I wondered as to how I was going to finish this book, I began to be reminded of Soren Kierkegaard's quotation (title of this final chapter).

Listening and watching the proceedings on television, listening to President Biden talk, and looking at the shape of this inauguration ceremony, it dawned on me that this book foreshadowed the message of this inauguration day.

President Biden began the day by attending Mass. He clearly has faith in God. He spoke of the present crises in the USA as being a time of opportunity. He spoke of friendship and how we must work together in harmony. He defended truth and spoke ill of lies and false promises... *to defend the truth and to defeat the lies*[135]... the serpent of Eden was definitely not happy! The stars came out and sang... namely Lady Gaga, Jennifer Lopes and Garth Brooks. Indeed Brooks sang *Amazing Grace*. Biden continued by saying all humans must be treated with dignity, and love. He mentioned the planet and the need to deal with global warming... *a cry for survival comes from the planet itself*[136]... He spoke of change, or metanoia. He mentioned binding up past wounds and achieving great things by taking many small steps, starting with the first step, on a journey returning to a state of normality. He spoke of preserving, defending

---

[135]www.telegraph.co.uk/news/0/joe-biden-inauguration-speech-full-transcript-2021-president/

[136] Ibid

and protecting the constitution of the USA. President Biden humbly asked the good people of America to help him on his journey... this humility clearly showed that he firmly believed that he did not own America. Finally, President Biden was full of hope and his hope was inclusive of all Americans no matter what their creed, colour or politics was, as he pleaded with them to open their souls instead of holding a hardness of heart, as they journeyed together towards a sustainable harvest.

The following day, President Biden announced that the USA was rejoining the Paris agreement promoting sustainability, and rejoining the World Health Organisation, (WHO)... (President Trump, during his time in office had decided to leave both movements/ organisations).

This book places the God of creation at its centre. The importance of human dignity is stressed, especially the importance of treating the poor of the Third World with dignity. The genesis of the seeds which lead to dark human nature are traced, dark nature that can be overcome through friendship, love, kindness, truth, honesty, faith in God, prayer and faith in basic good human nature. This book is interested in preserving, defending and protecting this beautiful planet through the grace of God, other world religions/beliefs or through philosophical humanistic thought. It underlines the fact that we do not own the planet. Star singers were not invited to perform during the journey, however the crux of its message is written in the stars. Hope is present in this story, as we request the intersession of Our Lady of Holy Hope. Finally, all humanity is invited to journey on a path less travelled, no matter what their belief system is, no matter what their bank balance is.

On the subject of hope, I was reminded one day, as I listened to a discussion on the topic on the Ryan Tubridy show[137], how prayer and spirituality is a diminishing aspect of our lives and of our coping mechanism in today's pandemic dominated world. Unfortunately, my sentiment of Chapter 11 seems to be gaining a stronger footing as the months and years pass by, i.e. we live in a "post religion post truth" world.

Religion exists side by side with spirituality, and I feel some people are simply gone too materialistic, in their efforts to experience Hope, in this sometimes hopeless world of lockdowns and worry driven by the on-going Covid-19 crisis...these people clearly lack spirituality.

I also feel that truth suffers where spirituality is lacking.

Personally, I very much believe in religion and spirituality and in the Novena to Our Lady of Holy Hope, (Chapter 11), because I have seen and experienced the fruits of this intersessionary prayer.

To conclude, my hope is that humanity will move forward with purpose and hope in the years to come.

In the realisation that within the world of spirituality philosophy exists, I do feel confident that we will somehow find a way.

In the spirit of metanoia or change of heart, may we change our collective lifestyles by reducing our personal carbon footprint (reducing our own personal standard of living), as we joyfully journey towards a sustainable planet (a planet whose resources we treat with respect in the realisation that we do not own it).

---

[137] RTE radio 1, Republic of Ireland

Finally... a thought for our mythological/theological parents... the central characters of this story.

Many years ago, at the birth of the Cosmos *they found each other*[138], and had a potential beautiful life together. A lot has happened since... including God casting them from Eden[139]. However, it is my firm belief that God never left their side, as they tilled the soil and suffered the various hardships of life outside of Eden.

From time to time, as I look at the night sky over the Galtee Mountains in County Tipperary, I sometimes think of them as they peacefully stand in friendship and harmony (based on love), with Judas and all the souls in Heaven.

I hope that they will once again smile blissfully, as they once did in the original *very good*[140] creation that was Eden, when they notice definite positive signs indicating that we are beginning to gradually experience healing within our collective human hearts. Healing that will encourage us to work together in harmony, as we journey onwards, free from the scourge of mob mentality and connected with our state of nature, on a pathway leading towards a sustainable planet, which will reflect the once perfect Garden of Eden.

---

[138] Tyldum, M., and Spaihts, J.

[139] Gen. 3:23

[140] Gen. 1:31

EPILOGUE

I took a drive to the Glen of Aherlow on the night of the first Sunday in September 2021. It was a dry very mild autumn night. The sky was clear, and the stars danced joyfully and spectacularly in the Heavens. The plough was clearly seen over the Galtees.

I parked my car, turned off the lights and engine, rolled down the window, and listened... listened to the sound of nature.

Many thoughts came flooding back to my mind and heart... thoughts of moments spent here as a child with my parents and brother and sisters... warm carefree days that have now become precious memories.

Another thought that entered my mind was a recent conversation I had with a friend regarding WhatsApp. He asked me if I was on WhatsApp. I replied, "no I am not, and I have no intention of ever being on WhatsApp"... I continued by saying... "if I had got a Euro each time I had been asked that question over the past few years, I would be a very wealthy man".

Then my thoughts returned to the present and the sad reality of global warming. The shocking reality of a continual rise in CO_2 e emissions worldwide was forefront in my mind and on my heart, along with the terrible problem of plastic waste in the form of waste packaging in Ireland. Ireland's waste plastic and paper from packaging has increased by 11% between 2018-2019[141].

The Irish Government recently announced a new housing scheme... affordable social housing for all... while the term sustainable was used in the documentation. In my opinion, there is nothing sustainable about the proposed design and materials planned to be used in the construction of these houses[142].

Ryanair, the Irish aviation company has recently published very optimistic growth projections... (September 2021). Pre-Covid-19 they had 149 million passengers... by March 2026 they predict that they will have 225 million passengers... 25 million more than their previous target of 200 million[143].

The Covid-19 problem is getting worse in the Third World, especially in Africa[144], and this reality is sadly no longer making major news headlines worldwide.

Globally, we are not in a good place.

Dolores O'Riordan (RIP) of the Cranberries[145] would be celebrating her 50th birthday this week, if she was still alive, (6th September 2021). Instead she is in Heaven tonight looking down on all of us.

---

[141] www.thejournal.ie/packaging-waste-one-million-tonnes-ireland-recycling-epa-5544816-Sep2021/

[142] www.gov.ie/en/press-release/ee5a9-government-launches-housing-for-all-a-new-housing-plan-for-ireland/

[143] www.travelweekly.co.uk/news/air/ryanair-upgrades-post-pandemic-growth-projections

[144] www.bloomberg.com/news/articles/2021-09-09/africa-variants-may-derail-global-covid-19-fight-scientists-say

[145] www.cranberries.com

Dolores' mother was interviewed on the Late Late show last Friday night, (3rd September 2021).

During the interview with Ryan Tubridy, she described her lovely daughter as being a very honest child growing up... a child of *incredible honesty*[146]. Dolores the honest child became a truthful honest young woman.

Dolores O'Riordan retained the innocence, purity, honesty and truthfulness of a child, as she grew into adulthood... she was not affected or changed in a negative way by society, or the monetary gain her outstanding singing talent provided her with.

Tonight, as I gaze at the stars over the Galtee Mountains, I am well aware that Adam, Eve, Judas and all the souls, (of which Dolores O'Riordan is one), of the very good people who walked this planet before we did... who did their very best... saving hay, tilling the soil, playing music, singing, playing sport, rearing families, and doing other chores... gaze down on us... on all of us, no matter where we live.

Tonight, with this in my mind and on my heart, I make one plea to all who will read this book in the years to come...

Please do something in your life to reduce the effects of global warming that threatens this beautiful planet... even if it has to involve a reduction in your own personal standard of living ... something that will bring a blissful smile to the faces of all the souls in Heaven.

---

[146] www.evoke.ie/2021/09/04/evoke/late-late-show-viewers-praise-powerful-tribute-to-late-dolores-oriordan-from-her-mum

If this happens with regularity, we will be on the correct pathway towards creating a sustainable planet.

As for the other pathway... it is not worth contemplating.

Tonight, October 19th 2021, I once again sit typing in my study. The temperature in Tipperary Town reached 20°C today and the present night-time temperature outside is 10°C.

I then proceeded to look up some historical weather data, collected in Dublin Airport during the month of October 1975.

Using this data, I calculated the average minimum temperature and maximum temperature for October in Dublin forty six years ago.[147]

My results were as follows:

Average minimum temperature = 7.5°C.

Average maximum temperture = 12.9°C.

Our current crisis of global warming can be instantly seen.

Our night-time temperature has risen by approximately (10.0 - 7.5) = 2.5°C.

Our day-time temperature has risen by approximately (20.0 - 12.9) = 7.1°C.

These statistics are worrying.

In my opinion it is plain to see that this trend needs to be arrested.

---

[147]https://weatherspark.com/h/m/147697/1975/10/Historical-Weather-in-October-1975-at-Dublin-Airport-Ireland

A Journey Towards Sustainability

The future of this planet depends on us... on our collective choices.

This journey towards sustainability, which began in Eden, will end some day, as all journeys do.

Where it ends is entirely in our collective hands.

It will depend on the choices we make.

And those choices will be made by you and me.

ABOUT THE AUTHOR

Miley's meadow summer 2021

Tommy Treacy began his career working as a QC technician in Merck Sharp & Dohme, and teaching for a period of time in the Vocational School Clonmel.

After five years in St Patrick's College Maynooth he was ordained Deacon and ministered in the Irish dioceses of Cork & Ross and Waterford & Lismore.

Tommy currently works in Griffith College Limerick, where he lectures in Advanced Manufacturing Technology and Sustainability.

The experiences gained on this journey, has inspired Tommy to write this book.

PLEASE REVIEW

Dear Reader,

If you found this book helpful, would you kindly post a short review on Amazon or Goodreads? Your feedback will make all the difference to getting the word out about this book.

To leave a review, go to Amazon and type in the book title. When you have found it go to the book page, please scroll to the bottom of the page to where it says 'Write a Review' and then submit your review.

Thank you in advance.

REFERENCES

Ainger, C., Fenner, R. (2014) *Sustainable Infrastructure: Principles into Practice.* London, ICE Publishing.

Barrett, M. (2008) *Crossing Reclaiming the Landscape of Our Lives.*, 2nd edn. London, Darton, Longman & Todd Ltd.

Berners-Lee, M. (2010*) How Bad Are Bananas?* London, Profile Books Ltd.

Bhaktivedanta Swami Prabhupada, A. C., His Divine Grace (1983) *Bhagavad-Gita As It Is.* London, The Bhaktivedanta Book Trust.

Boadt, L., (1984) *Reading The Old Testament An Introduction.* New York, Paulist Press.

Brodd, J. and Sobolewski, G. (2003) *World Religions, A Voyage of Discovery,* 2nd edn. Winona, Saint Mary's Press, Christian Brothers Publications.

Brown, R., E., Fitzmyer, J., A., and Murphy, R., E. (2000) *The New Jerome Biblical Commentary.* London, A Continuum Imprint.

Catechism of the Catholic Church. (1994) Dublin, Veritas Publications.

Cox, B. and Cohen, A. (2014) *Human Universe.* London, William Collins Publisher.

Cox, B. and Cohen, A. (2011) *Wonders of The Universe.* London, Harper Collins Publishers.

Cronin, C., Tiernan, S. (2015) *Breaking Ground*, 2nd edn. Dublin, Ed Company of Ireland.

Dawkins, R. (2011) *The Magic of Reality*. London, Bantam Press.

Descartes, R. (1649) *The Passions of the Soul*. Indianapolis, Hackett Publishing Company.

Egan, B. *Sunday Independent Living 6/9/2020*. Dublin, Sunday Independent.

Egan, B. *Sunday Independent Sport 21/6/2020*. Dublin, Sunday Independent.

Everett, B., Boyle G., Peake, S., and Ramage, J. (2012) *Energy Systems and Sustainability Power for A Sustainable Future,* 2nd edn. Oxford, Oxford University Press.

Francis, Pope. (2015) *Laudato Si' (Praised Be)*. Dublin, Veritas Publications.

Government of Ireland (2021) *Climate Action and Low Carbon Development (amendment) Bill 2021.*

Green, W. (2012) *Jim Stynes My Journey*. Dublin, Penguin Ireland.

Gribbin, J. (2006) *The Universe A Biography*. London, The Penguin Group.

Harris, D., C., (2010) *Quantitative Chemical Analysis*, 8th edn. New York, W. H. Freeman and Company.

Hawking, S., (2018) *Brief Answers To The Big Questions*. London, John Murray (Publishers).

Helm, D. (2015) *The Carbon Crunch*. London, Yale University Press.

Hone, D. (2017) *Putting the Genie Back*. Bingley, Emerald Publishing Ltd.

https://weatherspark.com/h/m/147697/1975/10/Historical-Weather-in-October-1975-at-Dublin-Airport-Ireland

Inch, A. M. (2002) *Whispers of Heaven & Heaven according to Matthew*. Fairfax VA, Xulon Press USA.

Kennedy, D. (2014) *Chemistry Live,* 2nd edn. Dublin, Folens Publishers.

Kennelly, B. – *Poetry Archive*.

Kung, H. (2007) *The Beginning of All Things Science and Religion*. Michigan, Wm. B. Eerdmans Publishing Co.

Lawlor, D. (2013) *Lar Corbett All In My Head*. London, Transworld Ireland Publishers Ltd.

Le Quere, C., Jackson, R.B., Jones, M.W., et al. (2020) *Temporary reduction in daily global CO_2 emissions during COVID 19 forced confinement, Nature Climate Change.*

Lefteri, C., (2016) *Making It Manufacturing Techniques for Production Design*, 3rd edn. London, Laurence King Publishing.

library.timelesstruths.org/music/Beautiful_Isle_of_Somewhere//

Magee, B. (2001) *The Story of Philosophy*. London, Dorling Kindersley Ltd.

Matthews, R. (1993) *Unravelling the Mind of God*, 2nd edn. London, Virgin Publishing Ltd.

Maull, A., F., (2015) *A Universal Vision of Human Goodness and Social Transformation*. Claritas, Journal of Dialogue & Culture, Vol 4, No. 2.

Mautner, T. (2000) *The Penguin Dictionary of Philosophy,* 4th edn. London, Penguin Books Ltd.

Mullins, M. (2003) *The Gospel of John, A Commentary*. Dublin, The Columba Press.

O'Shea, J. (2011) *ABUSE Domestic Violence, Workplace and School Bullying*. Cork, Atrium, Cork University Press.

O'Sullivan, K. and McGee H., (2021) *The Irish Times.* Dublin, 24-28 Tara Street.

Our Lady of Holy Hope Novena Prayer. Parish of Cahir, Diocese of Waterford & Lismore Ireland, Thursday May 4th 2017.

Peck, M., S. (1983) *The Road Less Travelled.* Reading, Cox & Wyman Ltd.

Phelan, C. *The Irish Daily Mirror 30/11/2021.* Dublin, 27 - 32 Talbot Street.

Quinlan, H., E. (2020) *Plagues, Pandemics, and Viruses, From The Plague Of Athens To Covid-19.* Canton, Visible Ink Press.

Roshitsh, K. (2021) *Sustainability a new American value in Inauguration speeches.*

Schwab, K. (2016) *The Fourth Industrial Revolution: what it means, how to respond.*

shop.gavinjamesmusic.com

Springsteen, B. (2016) *Born to Run.* London, Simon & Schuster UK Ltd

St. Paul's letter to the Ephesians. 2: 8

St. Paul's letter to the Romans. 3: 23; 8: 19

St Paul's second letter to the Thessalonians. 2: 8

Stein, J., Bock, J., and Harnick, S. *Fiddler on the Roof.* London, Weinberger Ltd.

Stoanes, C., Stevenson, A., (2006) *Concise Oxford English Dictionary*, 11th edn. Oxford, Oxford University Press.

Strain, D.T., (2013) *The Role of Philosophy in Spirituality.*

Tavakoli, A., *How Precisely Kaya Identity can estimate GHG Emissions: A Global review.* University of Zanjan. Iran.

The Book of Genesis. 1: 1-10; 1: 31; 2: 25; 3: 3; 3: 4-5; 3: 7; 3: 8; 3: 19

The Book of Revelation. 21: 23

The Book of Wisdom. 2:24; 11:26

The Divine Office Volume II, Daily Prayer for Lent and Eastertide. A reading from an ancient homily for Holy Saturday, Holy Saturday office of readings.

The Gospel of St John. 3: 8; 8: 32; 18: 37: 18: 38

The Gospel of St Matthew. 6: 26; 26: 75; 27: 3-4

The Harper Collins Study Bible. London, Harper Collins Publishers.

Thunberg, G., (2019) *No One Is Too Small To Make A Difference.* London, Penguin Random House UK.

Tyldum, M., and Spaihts, J. (2016) *Passengers.* Sony Pictures Entertainment, Columbia Pictures.

Walsh, T., F. *More Favourite Poems We Learned in School.* Dublin, Mercier Press.

Wheatley, M., J. (2002) *Silence is the problem.* Shambhala Sun.

Wright, I. (2019) *dynamics of stillness.* London, Eddison Books Ltd.

www.azlyrics.com/lyrics/lesmiserablescast/onedaymore.html

www.bbc.com/news/world-europe-53429064

www.bloomberg.com/news/articles/2021-09-09/africa-variants-may-derail-global-covid-19-fight-scientists-say

www.britannica.com/technology/carbon-offset

www.britannica.com/technology/flue-gas-treatment

www.christianity.com/bible/commentary/matthew-henry-concise/genesis/3

www.christianitytoday.com/news/2021/october/ireland-abortion-pro-life-christian-politics-repeal-covid.html

www.clarelibrary.ie/eolas/coclare/people/parnell.htm

www.collinsdictionary.com/dictionary/english/at-a-loss

www.collinsdictionary.com/dictionary/english/to-be-singing-from-the-same-hymn-sheet

www.comment.org/jesus-is-a-jew/

www.cranberries.com

www.curious.earth/blog/greta-thunberg-quotes-best-21/

www.etymonline.com/word/crux

www.evoke.ie/2021/09/04/evoke/late-late-show-viewers-praise-powerful-tribute-to-late-dolores-oriordan-from-her-mum

www.famvin.org/en/2020/09/28/to-love-another-person-is-to-see-the-face-of-god-part-i/

www.france24.com/en/20181006-pope-says-church-can-no-longer-tolerate-silence-abuse

www.genius.com/David-bowie-space-oddity-lyrics

www.globeatnight.org/mythology/crux

www.gov.ie/en/press-release/ee5a9-government-launches-housing-for-all-a-new-housing-plan-for-ireland/

www.healthline.com/health/repressed-emotions

www.independent.ie/news/environment/pollution-from-smokeless-coal-fire-as-bad-as-smoky-fuels-39358700.html

www.investopedia.com/terms/c/carbontrade.asp

www.irishexaminer.com/sport/gaa/arid-40043561.html

www.irishtimes.com/culture/books/philosopher-of-the-heart-review-kierkegaard-s-existential-angst-1.3831689

www.irishtimes.com/culture/music/bruce-springsteen-to-play-croke-park-concert-in-may-1.2522291

www.irishtimes.com/news/environment/carbon-emissions-down-last-year-by-just-3-6-despite-covid-19-restraints-1.4707194

www.irishtimes.com/news/ireland/irish-news/government-is-warned-of-high-cost-of-not-achieving-climate-action-plan-1.4035349

www.irishtimes.com/news/world/amazon-fires-brazilian-states-ask-for-military-help-amid-record-blazes-1.3996476

www.ivypanda.com/essays/holy-spirit-in-todays-world-theology/

www.macmillandictionary.com/us/dictionary/american/the-heart-crux-of-the-matter

www.merriam-webster.com/dictionary/crux

www.merriam-webster.com/dictionary/covenant

www.merriam-webster.com/dictionary/intimate

www.mirror.co.uk/3am/celebrity-news/david-bowie-didnt-fear-death-7169844

www.nasa.gov/topics/history/features/apollo_8.html

www.newgrange.com/winter_solstice.htm

www.nrcan.gc.ca/energy/publications/16226

www.nytimes.com/2020/04/09/world/coronavirus-equipment-rich-poor.html

www.nytimes.com/2020/07/22/world/asia/us-china-cold-war.html

www.planetary.org/worlds/pale-blue-dot

www.quotefancy.com/quote/1647944/Grey-Owl-Friends

www.rembrandtpaintings.com/judas-returning-the-thirty-pieces-of-silver.jsp

www.scientificamerican.com/article/coal-ash-is-more-radioactive-than-nuclear-waste/

www.scrippsco2.ucsd.edu/history_legacy/keeling_curve_lessons.html

www.sparknotes.com/philosophy/rousseau/themes/

www.stmaryscahir.webs.com

www.telegraph.co.uk/news/0/joe-biden-inauguration-speech-full-transcript-2021-president/

www.thejournal.ie/ireland-buying-carbon-credits-4681370-Jun2019/

www.thejournal.ie/ireland-carbon-credits-emissions-4901302-Nov2019/

www.thejournal.ie/packaging-waste-one-million-tonnes-ireland-recycling-epa-5544816-Sep2021/

www.time.com/person-of-the-year-2019-greta-thunberg/

www.toppr.com/ask/question/if-there-was-no-co2-in-the-earths-atmosphere-the-temperature-of-earths-surface-would-2/

www.travelweekly.co.uk/news/air/ryanair-upgrades-post-pandemic-growth-projections

www.waste360.com/plastics/plastics-manufacturing-and-greenhouse-gas-emissions-are-plastics-new-coal